I dedicate this book to my two pillars of strength,
my mother-in law, Leela Khatau and my mother, Sudha Sampat
and seek their blessings.

Epicure's

Vegetarian

Cuisines of

India

Epicure's

Vegetarian

Cuisines of

India

ASHA KHATAU

Popular
Prakashan

Popular Prakashan Pvt. Ltd.
35-C, Pt. Madan Mohan Malaviya Marg
Tardeo, Mumbai 400 034

First Publication 2003

(3865)

ISBN-81-7991-119-5

Photography by Mangesh Parab

Typeset and Designed
by Vans Information Ltd.
35-C, Pt. Madan Mohan Malaviya Marg
Tardeo, Mumbai 400 034.

Printed in India
by New Model Impex Pvt. Ltd, New Delhi
& Published by Ramdas Bhatkal
for Popular Prakashan Pvt. Ltd.
35-C, Pt. Madan Mohan Malaviya Marg
Tardeo, Mumbai 400 034.

AUTHOR'S NOTE

India is a vast and ancient land, with a recorded history that dates back over 3000 years. It is divided into 28 states and provinces that stretch from snowy mountains of Kashmir to the southern tip of Kerala and from the harsh deserts of Rajasthan in the west across to the remote tribal region of Assam. There are 114 different languages spoken all over the country. With all these differences, cuisines of India may seem indefinable, but there are common strands that weave together to form a thrilling tapestry. Its geographical conditions also affect the kind of grain used as staple food like wheat, rice, millet, maize, etc. Spices which are a foundation of Indian cookery are widely cultivated according to regions. The Indian kitchen's range of spices is hard to beat in terms of its variety, colour and aroma – from the sweetness of cumin, pungency of asafoetida and spice of chillies. The spices may be dried or fresh, full or ground or put in oil to expel the flavours. Some such as cardamom, cinnamon and saffron may be also used for desserts. Any combination of spices is referred to as *masala*.

The most widely used is *garam masala* — a fragrant combination of a dozen spices. The ancient Sanskrit treatise on Ayurveda – the Hindu science of medicine lists how different spices help to cure ailments in our body. For example, turmeric acts as an antiseptic, while pepper and chillies cure digestive ailments, ginger is for headaches, fevers and brain ailments. That is why the medicinal properties and the combinations of spices with vegetable, grain or pulse is always taken into account when food is prepared. All Indian food is served with either rice or bread or both. Food is generally served on a banana leaf or a *thali*. The traditional *thali* contains all the courses of meal. The sweet, which is milk based, completes the meal and also soothes the stomach.

The grand finale is the betel leaf known as the *paan*. Along with its seasoning, it is a digestive and gives a fitting finale to Indian hospitality. Washing of hands before meals is an important ritual, since Indians generally use their fingers to eat.

Indian cookery varies so widely from region to region, and from one cook to the other, that even the best known dishes have many variations. From olden times, cooking has been an art, a tradition handed down from ancestors. All instructions were oral or practically shown. (Well, that's how I have learned part of my cooking.) But, now, times have changed and we have cook books that help a lot of people in India and throughout the world and give easy guidelines about traditional food. As in any art, the personality and vision of an artist is reflected so also, Indian cooking, through the use of spices, expresses individuality and the special talent of a cook.

So here is an opportunity for all of you to explore the best you have in you with the help of this book. Keeping the present needs and requirements in mind, I have compiled this edition with some favourite and some unusual dishes. It also contains the best recipes from homes, restaurants and some traditional recipes from rural India. I wish you all the happiness and good eating with your family and friends while experimenting from this book.

Aham vaishva, Naro bhutva, Praninam deham aashritah, Prana pan samayukta, pacham myanam chaturvidham!

This is a traditional prayer in Sanskrit, recited before starting any meal. It invokes God to bless the food we eat and for better digestion. ENJOY!!!!

ACKNOWLEDGEMENTS

My sincere thanks to the One above....

Who made me capable and strong.

To all my elders who are no more with us but taught me a lot when they were around.

To my family...My husband Mahendra Khatau, who made me what I am today, and my 3 children-Priya, Shreya and Manish for their constant encouragement and support.

To my two pillars of strength – my mother-in-law Leela Khatau and my mother Sudha Sampat.

To my sister-in-law Ameeta Thackersey and brother-in-law Jagdish Thackersey for their special help and support all through out.

To a very special friend Rageshwari for her moral support.

To my sister Raksha, my friend Aditya Mahadevia and Madhu Ruia for their help in editing.

To my cousin Leena Thackersey, my friends Vandana Kejriwal and Kamal Ajmerwala for their help in the photo shoot.

To Harsha Bhatkal, Swapna Shinde and all of those at Popular Prakashan.

To special friends Jayakumar and Madhu to get the ball rolling for me at the publishing house.

To my dedicated staff at home, Gopinath, Mahadev, Vinod, Naresh and Dattu.

To all my close friends who cheered me on.

And lastly to all of you who bought my book and enjoy cooking for your family and friends.

Namaste........

CONTENTS

GUJARATI

MAHARASHTRIAN

NORTH INDIAN

SOUTH INDIAN

RAJASTHANI

BEST OF THE REST

HANDVO
Savoury Cake
┼┼┼┼┼┼┼┼┼┼┼┼┼┼┼┼┼┼┼┼┼┼┼┼

INGREDIENTS

For Handva Flour

Rice	¾ cup
Red split gram	½ cup
Yellow split gram	½ cup
Wheat	2 tbsps
Bengal gram	2 tbsps
White split gram	2 tbsps

(All ground together)

Sour yogurt	1 cup
Soda	½ tsp
Grated bottle gourd	1 cup
Oil	2-3 tbsps
Sugar	1 tsp
Ginger chilli paste	2 tsps
Fruit salt	1 tsp
Asafoetida	a pinch
Salt	to taste

For Tempering

Oil	4-5 tbsps
Mustard seeds	1 tsp
Sesame seeds	2 tsps
Round red chillies	3-4
Asafoetida	a pinch
Curry leaves	a few

METHOD

1. Soak *handva* flour mixture with sour yogurt and soda for six hours or overnight.
2. Grease a six cup sized baking dish with a little oil. Preheat the oven to 150°c. When the batter is fermented; add grated gourd salt, ginger-chilli paste, sugar, asafoetida, two tablespoons of oil and fruit salt like ENO and mix it with a little water.
3. Mix the batter very lightly and pour it into a greased baking dish.
4. Place the batter in the freezer until you get the tempering ready.
5. In a small vessel, heat four tablespoons of oil, add mustard and sesame seeds. When they splutter, add asafoetida, red chillies and curry leaves.
6. Remove the *handva* from the freezer and pour the tempering over the top and bake it in a preheated oven for twenty to twenty five minutes or until golden from top.
7. Remove from oven and cool. Cut into squares and serve with green *chutney* or sweet-sour pickle, accompanied by buttermilk.

Serves 6-8

BAJRI-METHI NA THEPLA
Millet and Fenugreek Bread
++

INGREDIENTS

Wheat flour	1 cup	Sour yogurt to bind the dough	
Millet flour	1 cup	Salt	to taste
Coriander powder	1 tsp	Oil	for shallow frying
Cumin powder	1 tsp	Turmeric powder	¼ tsp
Fresh fenugreek leaves	1 cup	Chilli powder	1 tsp
Oil	2 tbsps	Ginger-chilli paste ......)	1 tsp
Jaggery	2 tsps		

METHOD

1. Mix both the flours along with all the dry spices, fenugreek leaves and two tablespoons of oil. Bind semi-soft dough with the help of yogurt. Do not add water.
2. Divide the dough into twelve to fourteen balls. Roll out four to five inch thin circles with a rolling pin. Shallow fry the *theplas* over medium flame, using a little oil. Pour oil with a small spoon around the edge of the *thepla*.
3. Turn over and repeat the process. When they are cooked properly take it off and serve hot with vegetable, *chunda*, *raita* or as a teatime snack.

Makes 12-14

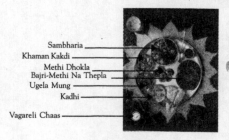

Sambharia
Khaman Kakdi
Methi Dhokla
Bajri-Methi Na Thepla
Ugela Mung
Kadhi

Vagareli Chaas

PANKI
Rice Pancakes Cooked in Banana Leaf
+++

INGREDIENTS

For the Panki

Rice flour	1½ cups	Salt	to taste
Sour yogurt	2 cups	Green chilli-ginger paste	1 tsp
Sugar	½ tsp	Oil	for cooking
Fenugreek seeds	½ tsp		

To Serve

Banana leaves cut into 6" x 6" squares .... 2 large

Green *chutney* and tempered green chillies (recipe given below)

METHOD

FOR THE PANKI

1. Place the rice flour in a large vessel; mix it with sour yogurt, sugar and fenugreek seeds. Mix thoroughly to make a smooth batter. Cover and keep overnight in a warm place. The batter should be fermented and sour.
2. Add chilli-ginger paste and salt to taste. Mix thoroughly.
3. Apply oil on the banana leaf, and keep aside.
4. Heat a frying pan or flat griddle and put a little oil in it.
5. Place one oiled leaf on it and pour three to four tablespoons of batter and spread evenly.
6. Cover it with another leaf with the oiled part inside and cover this with a deep vessel and let the *panki* cook for three to four minutes. After it rises it should look like a light pancake and should be set with bubbles. Turn over and cook the other side as well.
7. Serve hot, straight from the banana leaf into the plate, along with the green *chutney* and green chillies.

FOR THE GREEN CHUTNEY

INGREDIENTS

Coriander leaves, washed and roughly chopped	1 bunch	Sugar	1 tsp
Green chillies, chopped	2-3 pieces	Roasted split gram	1 tbsp
Ginger	1inch piece	Juice of 1 lemon	
Cumin seeds	½ tsp	A pinch of asafoetida	

METHOD

Place all the ingredients in a *chutney* grinder with a little water and grind to a smooth paste. You can also grind it on an old traditional stone. Keep it in the fridge until ready to serve.

FOR TEMPERED CHILLIES (1)

INGREDIENTS

Ghee or oil .... 2 tbsps
Mustard seeds .... 1 tsp
Fenugreek seeds .... 1 tsp
Asafoetida .... a pinch

Green chillies, deseeded and chopped into ¼ inch
pieces 3-4
Rock salt .... ¼ cup
Cumin seeds .... 1 tsp

METHOD

1. Heat *ghee* or oil in a small vessel and put in the mustard and fenugreek seeds.
2. When they start spluttering, add cumin seeds and asafoetida.
3. Add chopped chillies and fry for five minutes, until soft. Add rock salt and mix well. Cool and serve.

Serves 6-8

FOR TEMPERED CHILLIES (2)

INGREDIENTS

Ghee .... 2 tbsps
Green chillies with stem, washed and halved .....
................................100 gms
Asafoetida ....1 tsp

Amchoor .... 1 tsp
Roasted cumin powder .... 1 tsp
Juice of 1 lemon
Salt .... to taste

METHOD

1. Heat *ghee* in a small pan and add asafoetida and chillies to it.
2. Cook until the chillies are slightly soft.
3. Add the remaining ingredients and cook for three to four minutes. Ensure that the spices do not get burnt.
4. Remove from the stove and cool. Serve as an accompaniment to any savoury dish.

Makes ½ cup

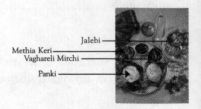

Jalebi
Methia Keri
Vaghareli Mirchi
Panki

BAJRI-METHI NI PURI
Millet-Fenugreek Crisps

INGREDIENTS

Fenugreek leaves, freshly chopped	½ cup	Sesame seeds	1 tsp
Millet flour	1 cup	Ginger-chilli paste	1 tsp
Oil	1 tsp	Turmeric powder	½ tsp
Salt	to taste	Flour	to roll
Black pepper	1 tsp	Oil	for frying
Garlic (chopped)	1 tsp		

METHOD

1. Chop fenugreek leaves, sprinkle half a teaspoon of salt and set aside.
2. Mix together millet flour, one teaspoon of oil, salt, pepper, garlic, sesame seeds, ginger-chilli paste and turmeric.
3. Mix fenugreek leaves with flour mixture and make a semi-soft dough with water.
4. Divide the dough into small cherry sized balls. Take one ball at a time, place it on a floured surface and with the help of your palms, shape into big coin-sized *puris*.
5. Prick them with a fork and fry in hot oil over a medium flame, till crisp.
6. You could also place it in a greased oven tray and bake in a hot oven (150ºc) for fifteen minutes.
7. Serve with *chutney* or yogurt as a teatime snack. Store it in an airtight container.

Makes 18-20 puris

KAND NO HANDVO
Pink Yam Cake

++

INGREDIENTS

Pink yam, boiled and mashed ....1 kg
Potatoes, boiled and mashed.......................... 2
Thick yogurt...2-3 tbsps
Green peas, boiled and crushed............... 2 cups
Oil.. 2 tbsps
Green chilli-ginger paste.......................... 2 tbsps
Grated coconut....................................... 4 tbsps
Freshly chopped coriander .... 4 tbsps
Salt .... to taste
Sugar .... to taste
Juice of 1 lemon

For Tempering
Oil ....2 tbsps
Mustard seeds .... 1 tsp
Sesame seeds 1tsp
Round red chillies....................................4-5
Curry leaves ....a few
To Garnish
Freshly grated coconut and freshly chopped
coriander
To Serve
Coconut Sauce
A square or rectangular greased baking dish (8x10)

METHOD

1. Mix together mashed yam, potatoes and yogurt. Season with salt and lemon juice and set aside.
2. Heat two tablespoons of oil in a frying pan, fry ginger-chilli paste briefly. Add green peas, sugar, salt and the remaining lemon juice to it. Remove from heat, add coconut and coriander and let it cool.
3. Spread half of the yam and potato mixture in a baking dish. Layer and spread the green pea mixture spread evenly.
4. Make a shape of the baking dish from the remaining yam mixture on a flat surface, and then spread this over the green pea. Mix and press to form a neat top.

FOR TEMPERING

1. Heat oil in a small pan, add mustard and sesame seeds, let them crackle, add chillies and curry leaves.
2. Spread the tempering over the yam mixture evenly and bake the mixture in a hot oven for fifteen to twenty minutes.
3. Let it rest for four to five minutes and then cut it into one inch by one inch square pieces and serve hot with green chutney or coconut sauce.

FOR THE COCONUT SAUCE

1. Heat one teaspoon of oil, add a pinch of cumin seeds and four-five curry leaves in it.
2. Add one cup of coconut milk to this mixture.
3. Add salt and sugar to taste. Serve warm or cold.

Serves 6-8

22

DAL DHOKLI
Whole Wheat Pasta Cooked in Split Gram Gravy
++

INGREDIENTS

For the Dal
Red split grams (*Toovar dal*) .... ½ cup
Turmeric powder .... ½ tsp
Raw peanuts .... 2 tbsps
Ginger .... 1inch piece
Asafoetida .... ½ tsp
Ginger-chilli paste .... 1 tbsp
Jaggery .... 2 tbsps
Mustard seeds .... ½ tsp
Kokam (black ones) .... 4-5 pieces
Ghee .... 2 tbsps
Curry leaves .... a few
Salt .... to taste

For the Dhokli
Whole-wheat flour .... ½ cup
Gram flour .... 1 tbsp
Ajwain .... ½ tsp
Turmeric powder .... ½ tsp
Red chilli powder .... ½ tsp
Salt .... to taste
Warm water .... to bind the dough
To Garnish
Finely chopped coriander leaves
To Serve
Finely chopped onions, green chillies and pieces of lemon.

METHOD

1. Wash and soak the gram in two cups of water for half an hour. Transfer this to the pressure cooker and add turmeric powder, peanuts, ginger and asafoetida to it.

2. Give three whistles to the cooker. Remove from heat and keep aside to cool. Bind the soft dough with the flours, *ajwain*, turmeric, chilli powder and salt, with the help of warm water.

3. Cover and set aside for half an hour. Divide the dough into six to eight portions. Roll each one into seven inch round circles with the help of a little flour.

4. Keep all of them on a paper separately, so that they do not stick to each other. Open the pressure cooker and lightly stir the gram with a wooden whisk in a large saucepan.

5. Heat *ghee* and add mustard seeds to it. When they splutter, add curry leaves and add the gram mixture. Add all the rest of the ingredients for the *dal* and let it simmer.

6. Mix all the ingredients together for the *dhokli* and make a soft dough. Divide into four to five balls.

7. Roll out each ball in seven to eight inches circles. Cut the circles into one inch long strips first and then cut each one diagonally to get diamond shaped pieces ten minutes before you want to serve.

8. When the gram mixture begins to boil add these pieces two-three at a time. Make sure each piece remains separate. Cook this for seven to eight minutes, till they are well cooked.

9. Garnish with coriander leaves. Serve at once with finely chopped onions, green chillies and lemon pieces.

Serves 6

MUNG NA DHOKLA
Green Gram Cake
+++

INGREDIENTS

Whole green gram, soaked for 6 hours ...... 1 cup

Coriander leaves, finely chopped .... 1 tbsp

Ginger-chilli paste .... 1 tbsp

Oil.. 1 tbsp

Fruit salt .... 1 tsp

Juice of ½ a lemon

Salt .... to taste

For Tempering

Oil.. 2 tbsps

Mustard seeds .... ½ tsp

Curry leaves 4-5

Asafoetida .... a pinch

To Garnish

3-4 tbsps of finely chopped coriander leaves and grated coconut

To Serve

Green *chutney* (recipe on page 19)

METHOD

1. Coarsely grind the green grams along with coriander leaves and water to a paste. The batter should not be too thick or thin.
2. Keep a wide vessel filled with water to boil and a metal ring at the bottom. Grease one stainless steel plate with a rim with oil and place it on the ring in boiling water.
3. To make the *dhokla*, mix together green gram paste, ginger-chilli paste, salt, one tablespoon of oil and fruit salt mixed with lemon juice.
4. Mix the batter lightly in circular movement, till all the ingredients are mixed properly. Pour this immediately into the greased plate over the boiling water. Cover tightly and steam for fifteen minutes. Remove from pan and set aside to cool slightly.

FOR TEMPERING

1. In a small vessel, heat oil, add mustard seeds and after they splutter add asafoetida and curry leaves to it.
2. Pour this over the steamed *dhokla*.
3. Garnish with coriander and coconut. Serve hot with green *chutney*.

Serves 4-6

BHAJI NA MUTHIA
Green Vegetable Dumplings
++

INGREDIENTS

Wheat flour	1 cup	Salt	1 tsp
Dark millet flour	¼ cup	Soda-bi-carbonate	a pinch
White millet flour	¼ cup	*For Tempering*	
Semolina	1 tbsp	Oil	1-2 tbsps
Gram flour	1 tbsp	Mustard seeds	½ tsp
Fenugreek	2 cups	Sesame seeds	½ tsp
Spinach leaves	2 cups	Asafoetida	½ tsp
Ginger-chilli paste	2 tbsps	Curry leaves	a few
Oil	2 tbsps	*To Garnish*	
Yogurt	2 tbsps	Grated fresh coconut and chopped coriander leaves	
Sugar	1 tsp	*To Serve*	
Sesame seeds	1 tsp	Green *chutney* (recipe on page 19)	

METHOD

1. In a large bowl, mix all the flours. Add the remaining ingredients and bind together a very soft dough.
2. Divide this into two or three parts and form cylindrical shapes. Place them in a greased steamer tray with holes. Cover and steam for thirty minutes.
3. Remove and set aside to cool. Cut them into half inch slices.
4. Heat oil in a frying pan for tempering. Add mustard and sesame seeds, when they splutter add asafoetida and curry leaves.
5. Arrange sliced dumplings over the tempering and heat them through. Turn over and cook the other side as well.
6. Remove on a serving plate, garnish with coconut-coriander and serve hot with green *chutney*.

Serves 6

METHI DHOKLA
Fenugreek Cakes

+++++++++++++++++++++++++++++++++++++

INGREDIENTS

Khaman dhokla mix (ready-made) .... 250 gms	Extra oil to grease the pan
Fenugreek leaves .... ½ cup	Small *idli* mould
Oil .... 1 tbsp	**To Serve**
Ginger-chilli paste .... 2 tsps	Coconut *chutney* (recipe on page 103)

METHOD

1. Empty the contents of the packet in a large bowl. Mix the washed fenugreek leaves, the satchet, oil and one and a half cups of water.
2. Mix thoroughly and spoon it into the greased *idli* mould and steam it in a covered vessel over hot water for fifteen minutes.
3. Remove with a sharp knife and serve hot with coconut *chutney*.

Makes 30 small idlies

(See photo on page 17)

EK TOAP NA DAL BHAAT
Rice And Split Gram Cooked In One Pan

╋╋╋

INGREDIENTS

Basmati rice, raw	2 cups	Tendli	200 gms
Red split gram	1 ½ cups	Fresh coriander, finely chopped	1 ½ cup
Yellow split gram	½ cup	Fresh coconut, grated	¾ cup
Ghee	¼ cup	Asafoetida	¼ tsp
Cloves	4-5	Sugar	1 tbsp
Cinnamon	1-2 pieces	Chilli-ginger paste	1 tbsp
Cardamom	3-4	Red chilli powder	½ tsp
Turmeric powder	¼ tsp	Coriander-cumin powder	1 tsp
Small sized potatoes	6-8	Gram flour, roasted	¼ cup
Small onions	10	Salt	to taste
Small brinjals	6-8	Juice of one lemon	

METHOD

1. Wash rice and both the grams separately. Soak rice for half an hour. In a big thick vessel heat *ghee* and add cloves, cinnamons and cardamoms.
2. After a minute, add turmeric, asafoetida and enough salt to the gram mixture. Mix well and add two cups of hot water. Cover and allow it to simmer till the grams are semi-cooked. Mix well coriander leaves, coconut, salt, sugar, asafoetida, turmeric powder, chilli powder, ginger-chilli paste, coriander-cumin powder, lemon juice and gram flour in a big plate.
3. Peel the potatoes and onions. Remove the stem from the brinjals and wash them. Put a vertical slit on both sides in all of them. Soak them in water.
4. Stuff the vegetables with the prepared spice mixture. Mix the remaining mixture with the vegetables so that they are well coated with the spices. Arrange them over the semi-cooked grams.
5. Add warm water as required to cook the vegetables. Cover and cook further.
6. When the vegetables are semi-cooked, evenly spread the rice over them. Add salt and a little *ghee* and enough warm water to cook the rice.
7. Cover and cook till done and until all the water evaporates.
8. Make sure the gram does not stick to the bottom. To serve, invert this over a large plate and serve hot with *kadhi*.

Serves 6-8

FADA NI KHICHDI
Cracked Wheat And Gram Mixture
+++

INGREDIENTS

Cracked wheat	1 cup	Cloves	3-4 pieces
Green split gram	½ cup	Turmeric powder	¼ tsp
Mixed vegetables, finely chopped	1 cup	Asafoetida	¼ tsp
Tomatoes, boiled and sieved	1½ cups	Chilli powder	½ tsp
Ginger	1inch piece	*Garam masala*	1 tsp
Salt	to taste	Ginger-chilli paste	1 tbsp
For Tempering		*To Serve*	
Ghee	3 tbsps	Spiced yogurt	
Cinnamon	1inch piece		

METHOD

1. Wash and soak cracked wheat and split gram separately for half an hour. Mix it with chopped vegetables, ginger and two cups of hot water. Pressure cook giving it three whistles. Set aside to cool.
2. After about twenty minutes open the cooker and churn the mixture with a wooden whisk to make the mixture even. Add a little hot water if the mixture is too dry in order to get a semi-soft consistency.
3. Add tomato puree and salt to taste and mix well. Transfer this to a heavy saucepan and put it on slow gas to simmer.
4. Heat *ghee* in a small saucepan and add all the tempering ingredients and let them sizzle.
5. Add this to the wheat mixture and mix well, beating vigorously.
6. Serve hot with spiced yogurt. (i.e. yogurt with salt, sugar, cumin powder, chilli powder and chopped coriander).

Serves 4-6

TRIRANGI BHAAT
Three Coloured Rice
+++

INGREDIENTS

For the Rice

Rice, washed and soaked	2 cups
Tomato purée	½ cup
Red chilli powder	1 tsp
Ghee or butter	4 tbsps
Turmeric powder	½ tsp
Yellow corn, boiled	½ cup
Cashews, chopped	2 tbsps
Medium onion, finely chopped	1
Juice of 1 lemon	
Salt	to taste

To Garnish
Fried onions and tomato slices

To Serve
Spiced Yogurt

Thick yogurt	2 cups
Oil	1 tbsp
Mustard seeds	1 tsp
Asafoetida	½ tsp
Dry red chillies (round ones)	2-3
Curry leaves	a few
Powdered sugar	1 tsp
Salt	to taste
Coriander, finely chopped	1 tbsp

METHOD

FOR THE RICE

The rice should be cooked with four cups of water in a way that each grain in separate. Divide the rice into three parts.

Red Layer: Mix together the tomato purée, salt and chilli powder. Add this to one part of the rice and set aside.

Yellow Layer: Heat one tablespoon of *ghee*. Add turmeric powder and corn. Fry for a minute and add the second part of rice and salt. Mix well and set aside.

White Layer: Heat one tablespoon of *ghee* and sauté the onions. When soft, add the cashews and fry for one more minute. Add the third part of the rice and salt and set aside.

To Assemble: Take a round baking dish. Apply *ghee* on all sides of the vessel. Put in the red rice. Spread it evenly by pressing it with your palm. Apply a little *ghee* on the layer. Spread the yellow and white rice in the same way. Bake in a hot oven (covered) for ten to twelve minutes. Invert it on a serving dish, garnish with onions and tomato slices. Serve hot with spiced yogurt. Alternatively, you can serve rice straight from the dish after baking, without inverting the dish.

FOR THE YOGURT

1. Beat the yogurt and set aside.
2. Heat oil in a small vessel. Add mustard seeds to it and when they start to splutter, add asafoetida, chillies and curry leaves.
3. Fry for half a minute and add this to the yogurt.
4. Add sugar, salt and coriander. Chill until ready to serve.

Serves 4-6

29

DUDHI NA THEPLA
Bread Made With Bottle Gourd

+++

INGREDIENTS

Wheat flour	1 cup	Ginger-chilli paste	1 tsp
Millet flour	1 cup	Coriander-cumin powder	1 tsp
Bottle gourd, grated	1 cup	Soda	a pinch
Oil	2 tbsps	Salt	to taste
Turmeric powder	¼ tsp	Sour yogurt to bind the dough	
Chilli powder	1 tsp	Oil for shallow-frying	

METHOD

1. Mix both the flours along with all the dry spices, bottle gourd, two tablespoons of oil and soda. Bind the semi-soft dough with the help of yogurt. Do not add water.
2. Divide the dough into twelve-fourteen balls. Roll out each one into flat, thin breads with a rolling pin.
3. Shallow fry the *theplas* over medium flame, using a little oil. Pour oil with a small spoon around the edge of the *thepla*. Turn over and repeat the process.
4. When they are cooked remove from heat and serve hot with *raita* or as a teatime snack.

Note :   *You could use Fenugreek leaves in place of bottle gourd.*

Makes 12-14

BHAKRI
Crisp Wheat Bread
+++++++++++++++++++++++

INGREDIENTS

Wheat flour .... 2 cups   Salt .... to taste
Ghee .... 6 tbsps

METHOD

1. Place the flour in a high-rimmed plate, make a well in the centre and add *ghee* and salt. Make the dough stiff with the help of water and set aside for half an hour.
2. Knead the dough once again to smooth and divide it into ten to twelve equal parts.
3. Roll out three inch round *rotis*. Roast on a griddle with a low flame. Flip the side and roast on the other side. Press the *bhakri* on the griddle in a circular movement with the help of a thick folded cloth or a wooden handled disc.
4. Turn over again and press to ensure that the *bhakri* is crisp and brown.
5. Serve hot.

Serves 6

PURIS
Puffed Unleavened Bread
+++++++++++++++++++++++

INGREDIENTS

Whole wheat flour, sieved .... 250 gms   Luke warm water .... ¼-½ cup
Ghee .... 2½ tbsps   Oil .... for frying

METHOD

1. Place flour in a deep bowl. Make a well in the center and pour *ghee* in it. Rub the flour till it starts looking like breadcrumbs. Add three tablespoons of warm water and rub the mixture with your fingertips.
2. Gather all the dough to form a round ball. Cover and set aside for thirty minutes. Divide the dough into twelve to fourteen small balls. Flatten each one and roll on a lightly floured surface. Roll to three to four inch rounds.
3. To fry immerse one *puri* at a time in hot oil. It will begin to puff up. Press it down gently with the back of a perforated spoon and cook for one minute. Turn it over and cook again for one more minute.
4. Drain on kitchen paper and serve hot with vegetables.

Makes 12-14 puries

SAMBHARIA
Stuffed Mixed Vegetable
++++++++++++++++++++++++++++++

INGREDIENTS

Small sized potatoes, peeled	250 gms	Sugar	2 tsps
Small onions, peeled	250 gms	Chilli powder	1 tsp
Small brinjals	250 gms	Juice of 1 lemon	
Tendli	100 gms	Salt	to taste
Rajiyani bananas	2	**For Tempering**	
Juice of 1 lemon		Green chillies, slit	2
Gram flour, roasted and mixed with 2 tbsps of oil		Mustard seeds	½ tsp
	1 cup	Fenugreek seeds	¼ tsp
Fresh coconut scraped	¾ cup	Oil	6 tbsps
Coriander leaves, finely chopped	½ cup	Curry leaves	a few
Coriander-cumin seed powder	1 tbsp	Asafoetida	¼ tsp
Ginger-chilli paste	1 tbsp		

METHOD

1. Put a vertical slit on one side of the potatoes and onions. Set aside in water. Remove the stem from the brinjals and slit. Cut both ends of the *tendli* and slit vertically.
2. Cut the bananas into two inch pieces and vertically slit them. Add coriander leaves, coriander-cumin seed powder, ginger-chilli paste to the gram flour and mix well. Stuff the mixture into the slits. Set the extra stuffing aside to sprinkle on top.
3. Heat oil in a large saucepan for tempering. Add chillies, mustard and fenugreek seeds to it. When they splutter, add curry leaves and asafoetida. Place all the vegetables except for the banana, and turn very gently in the pan.
4. Cover with a rimmed plate and put water in it. This will help the vegetables to cook on medium heat, and prevent the vegetables from sticking.
5. After twenty minutes when they are half cooked, remove the lid.
6. Add stuffed banana and the remaining mixture from the stuffing. Continue cooking on medium flame till the vegetables are tender. Take it off the flame, cover and set aside.
7. When you want to serve, turn the whole vegetable out on a deep serving platter and serve hot with *roti*.

Serves 6-8

(See photo on page 17)

BHARELA PARVAL NU SHAAK
Stuffed Parval Vegetable

++

INGREDIENTS

Parval, peeled and top and the bottom cap
removed .... 500 gms
Coriander leaves, finely chopped .... ½ cup
Fresh coconut scraped .... ½ cup
Peanuts, coarsely ground .... ¼ cup
Ginger-chilli paste .... 2 tbsps
Sugar .... 1 tsp
Garlic, crushed (optional) .... 1 tsp

Juice of 1 lemon
Salt .... to taste
For Tempering
Oil .... 1 tbsp
Cumin seeds .... 1 tsp
Green chillies 1-2
Curry leaves .... a few

METHOD

1. Slit the *parvals* from the middle without cutting them fully. Remove the seeds with a sharp knife, so as to create the hollow space in each one. Set aside.
2. In a medium sized bowl, mix together coriander leaves, fresh coconut grated, peanuts, ginger-chilli paste and sugar and stuff the hollow space in the *parval* with this mixture. Place them on a sieve over boiling water and steam them for fifteen to twenty minutes or until soft.
3. Remove from heat and set aside.
4. Heat oil in a frying pan, add cumin seeds, chillies and curry leaves. Add steamed *parvals* to it and mix very gently so that the *parvals* do not open out. Cook on a slow flame for five to seven minutes and serve hot with *rotis*.

Serves 4-6

TURIA-MAKAI NU SHAAK
Ridge Gourd and Corn Vegetable

++

INGREDIENTS

Oil .... 1 tbsp	Green chilli-ginger paste .... 2 tbsps
Cumin seeds .... ½ tsp	Sugar .... 1 tsp
Green chillies, slit 2-3	Thin coconut milk .... 2 cups
Curry leaves .... a few	Corn flour .... 1 tsp
Ridge gourd, skinned, slit vertically and cut	Tamarind water (optional) .... 1 tbsp
into 2 inch pieces .... 500 gms	Salt .... to taste
Soda .... a pinch	**To Garnish**
Corn kernels, boiled .... ½ cup	Finely chopped coriander .... 1 tbsp

METHOD

1. Heat oil in a heavy saucepan and add cumin seeds, chillies and curry leaves. Add chopped gourd, soda and a little water. Cook till they are soft.
2. Add boiled corn, chilli-ginger paste, sugar and coconut milk mixed with cornflour and salt to taste.
3. Let the mixture come to a boil and take it off the flame when thick. Add tamarind water (optional).
4. Garnish with coriander leaves and serve hot with *roti*.

<u>*Note*</u> :   *Make sure you don't overboil or else the coconut milk will curdle.*

Serves 4-6

GATHIA-MUTHIA NU SHAAK

Vegetable with Indian Savouries

+++

INGREDIENTS

For the Gathia

Gram flour	½ cup
Oil	1 tsp
Chilli powder	½ tsp
Ajwain	¼ tsp
Soda	a pinch
Salt	to taste
Oil	for frying

For the Muthia

Wheat flour	½ cup
Gram flour	½ cup
Fenugreek leaves, washed and chopped	½ cup
Oil	2 tbsps
Sugar	1 tsp
Chilli powder	1 tsp
Ginger-chilli paste	1 tbs
Turmeric powder	¼ tsp
Garam masala	½ tsp
Salt	to taste

For the Vegetable

Oil	2 tbsps
Mustard seeds	1 tsp
Fenugreek seeds	¼ tsp
Asafoetida	¼ tsp
Curry leaves	¼ tsp
Turmeric powder	¼ tsp
Chilli powder	1 tsp
Coriander powder	1 tsp
Cumin powder	1 tsp
Kokum	3-4 pieces
Jaggery	1 tbsp
Salt	to taste
Bottle gourd	½ kg
Potatoes, peeled and cubed	2
Green peas	½ cup
Fresh beans, cut into 1 inch long pieces and halved	100 gms
Water	2 cups
Salt	to taste

To Garnish

Finely chopped coriander leaves	3-4 tbsps
Coconut (scraped)	3-4 tbsps

METHOD

FOR THE GATHIA

1. Mix together gram flour, oil, chilli powder, *ajwain*, soda, salt and make a semi-soft dough adding some water. Cover and keep aside for half an hour.
2. Remove one-fourth of the dough and with the help of a little water, make it soft.
3. Roll this on a flat surface with both your palms to form a thick spaghetti like long *gathia*. Cut each one in two inch long sticks and fry them in hot oil till crisp.
4. Drain and set aside.

FOR THE MUTHIA

Mix all the ingredients together in a wide bowl and make a soft dough with little water. With the help of a little oil, shape these in one and half inch long dumplings, fry in hot oil, drain and set aside.

FOR THE VEGETABLES

1. Heat oil in a saucepan and add mustard and fenugreek seeds and when they splutter add asafoetida, curry leaves, and two cups of water. When the water begins to boil, add turmeric, chilli powder, and coriander-cumin powder. Now add all the vegetables.
2. Cook until the vegetables are soft. Then add jaggery and *kokum*. Add salt and bring to a boil. Just before serving add *gathia* and *muthia*. Garnish with coriander and coconut and serve hot.

Serves 4-6

BATATA NI KACHRI NU SHAAK
Vegetable of Potato Chips

++

INGREDIENTS

Potatoes, big sized	1 kg	Raisins	2-3 tbsps
Oil	3 tbsps	Turmeric powder	½ tsp
Mustard seeds	1 tsp	Chilli powder	1 tsp
Sesame seeds	2 tbsps	Dried mango powder	1 tsp
Peppercorns	6-8	Salt	to taste
Asafoetida	¼ tsp	Sugar	to taste
Round chillies	3-4	Oil	for frying
Curry leaves	finely chopped	**To Garnish**	
Cashew nuts, broken into pieces	2-3 tbsps	Coriander	finely chopped

METHOD

1. Cut potatoes into thin chips and soak them in cold, salted water for half an hour. Drain and place them on a thick cloth to dry. Fry them in hot oil till crisp and set aside.
2. Heat three tablespoons of oil in a wide pan and add mustard and sesame seeds.
3. When they splutter, add peppercorn, asafoetida, round chillies and curry leaves. Fry for half a minute, add cashew nuts and raisins and fry again.
4. Add fried potatoes along with turmeric powder, chilli powder, mango powder, salt and sugar to taste. Mix thoroughly. Garnish with coriander leaves and serve with hot *puris*.

Serves 6

DAHIWALI FANSI
French Beans in Yogurt

++

INGREDIENTS

French beans, cleaned and cut into 1 cms pieces .... ½ kg
Soda .... a pinch
Oil .... 3 tbsps
Mustard seeds .... ½ tsp
Asafoetida .... ¼ tsp
Green chillies 2-3
Chilli powder .... ½ tsp
Salt .... to taste
Sugar .... 1 tsp
Yogurt, beaten .... 2 cups
Cashewnuts, halved .... 10-12 pieces
Curry leaves .... a few
Coriander, finely chopped .... 2 tbsps

METHOD

1. Drop chopped French beans in boiling water adding a pinch of soda. Boil for seven to eight minutes. Drain and set aside. Heat two tablespoons (in a large frying pan) of oil and add mustard seeds.
2. When they splutter, add asafoetida and green chillies. Add boiled French beans salt and chilli powder. Cook until French beans are completely soft.
3. Let it cool completely. Add salt and sugar to the yogurt and add the cooled French beans. Mix well in a serving bowl.
4. Heat one tablespoon of oil (in a small tempering vessel) and add cashewnuts and curry leaves. Pour this over the French beans and sprinkle coriander on top and chill for two hours or until ready to serve.

Serves 4-6

KANDA-METHI NU SHAAK
Fenugreek-Onion Vegetable

+++

INGREDIENTS

Oil .... 3-4 tbsps
Green chilli, slit 1
Onions, chopped into small cubes .... 500 gms
Fenugreek leaves, freshly plucked and roughly chopped .... 1 bundle
Turmeric powder .... ¼ tsp
Chilli powder .... ½ tsp
Jaggery .... 1 tbsp
Salt .... to taste

METHOD

1. Heat oil in a frying pan and add chilli powder and onions. Fry till onions are semi-cooked. Sprinkle a little water if it sticks to the pan.
2. Add fenugreek leaves, salt, turmeric powder and chilli powder. Cook until both the vegetables are completely soft. Add jaggery and take it off the stove. Serve hot with *rotis*.

Serves 4-6

UNDHIYU
Stuffed Vegetables Surti Style
++++++++++++++++++++++++++++++++++++

INGREDIENTS

Surti papdi, without seeds	½ kg	Ginger	5 tbsps
Papdi seeds	¼ kg	Green garlic, finely chopped	1 bundle
Pink yam (Round variety)	½ kg	Green chillies, finely chopped	12
Fresh green lentils	100 gms	Salt	to taste
Potatoes	¼ kg	Sugar	to taste
Sweet potatoes (small sized)	4-5 pieces	Juice of 2 lemons	
Onions	¼ kg	*Garam masala* (optional)	2 tsps
Small brinjals	¼ kg	Fenugreek *muthia*	12 pieces
Tendli	¼ kg	Oil	½ cup
Rajeyani banana	3	*Ajwain*	½ tsp
Coriander leaves, finely chopped	1 ½ cup	Baking soda	1 tsp
Coconut, freshly grated	1 ½ cup	**To Garnish**	
Yellow fresh turmeric finely chopped	5 tbsps	Chopped coriander and scraped coconut	
Amba haldi	5 tbsps		

METHOD

1. Clean and wash *papdi* and peel it. Apply soda to it and set aside. Slightly crush the *tuver dana*. Peel the skin of *yam* and cut into big pieces.

2. Peel the potatoes, sweet potatoes and onions and stem brinjals. Soak all these vegetables in water. Wash *tendli* and snip the top and the bottom end.

3. Wash bananas and cut them into halves. Slit all the vegetables from both ends and keep them in water till they are ready to use. In a large plate mix together crushed *tuver*, coriander, coconut, both the turmeric, ginger, garlic and chillies.

4. Lightly toss them to mix. Add salt, sugar, lemon juice and *garam masala*. Mix well. Stuff into the slits of all the vegetables. Take potatoes, onions, *tendli*, sweet potato and banana and stuff the above mixture in the slits of each one reserving some to be sprinkled on top.

5. Heat oil in a large heavy saucepan and add *ajwain* and the *papdi* along with *papdi dana*.

6. Cook them until soft. Remove from the pan and set aside. In the same oil, place all the stuffed vegetables along with pink yam in layers. Carefully place then on top of each other so that the stuffing remains intact.

7. Cover and cook this until semi-soft. Now add the cooked *papdi* and the remaining *masala* of the stuffing. Cover and cook further until all the vegetables are completely soft. Serve hot with *puries* or *parathas*.

Note : Just before serving or before reheating the vegetables a little milk is added to enhance the flavour of the spices.

Serves 8-10

KADHI
Yogurt Soup
+-+-+-+-+-+-+-+-+-+-+-+-+-+-+-+-+

INGREDIENTS

For the Kadhi

Sour yogurt	2 cups
Water	4 cups
Gram flour	6 tbsps
Sugar	2-3 tbsps
Salt	1 ½ tbsp
Asafoetida	¼ tsp
Ginger-chilli paste	1 tbsp
Fresh coriander leaves	

Cumin seeds	1 tsp
Mustard seeds	1 tsp
Fenugreek	½ tsp
Cinnamon	1-2 sticks
Cloves	3-4
Red round chillies	3-4
White radish, cut long	6-8 pieces
Curry leaves	a few

For Tempering

Ghee .... 1 tbsp

METHOD

1. Combine all the ingredients for the *kadhi* and beat well with an eggbeater or wooden beater.
2. Heat *ghee* in a small vessel, add the cumin, mustard and fenugreek seeds.
3. Heat remaining tempering ingredients. After half a minute, pour it into the *kadhi*. Put the *kadhi* vessel on heat and let it boil.
4. Stir it often enough to avoid lumps from forming. Serve hot with coriander leaves sprinkled over it.

Serves 6-8

(See photo on page 17)

39

GOL KOKAM NI KADHI
Sweet and Sour Yogurt Soup

++

INGREDIENTS

Sour yogurt	1 ½ cups	Mustard seeds	½ tsp
Gram flour	4 tbsps	Fenugreek seeds	½ tsp
Split gram water	4 cups	Cumin seeds	½ tsp
Jaggery	3-4 tbsps	Asafoetida	½ tsp
Black *kokum*	3-4	Round red chillies	3-4
Ginger-Chilli paste	2 tsps	Curry leaves	a few
Salt	to taste	Brinjals, cubed	2 (small)
Ghee	2 tbsps	White radish, sliced into long strips 2 inch piece	

METHOD

1. Mix yogurt and flour with *dal* water and churn properly to avoid lumps. Add jaggery, *kokum*, ginger-chilli paste and salt.
2. Boil this mixture on medium heat, stirring occasionally. In another small pan, heat *ghee* and add mustard, fenugreek seeds and cumin seeds.
3. When they splutter, add asafoetida, round red chillies and curry leaves.
4. Add brinjal and radish and cook until the vegetables are soft. Now add this tempering to the yogurt mixture and bring to a boil. Simmer it for fifteen to twenty minutes. Serve hot with rice and thick yellow split gram (*lachko dal*).

Serves 6-8

LACHKO DAL
Thick Yellow Split Gram

++++++++++++++++++++++++++++++++++++++

INGREDIENTS

Red split gram	1 cup	Ghee	1 tbsp
Ginger	1 inch piece	Salt	to taste
Turmeric powder	¼ tsp	Asafoetida	¼ tsp

METHOD

1. Pressure-cook the red split gram with four to five cups of water, ginger, and turmeric powder. Give it three to four whistles. When cool, remove and drain out the water in another bowl which can be used for *kadhi* or *osaman*.
2. Heat *ghee* in a small pan. Add asafoetida and pour this over the cooked split gram.
3. Churn the cooked gram to a smooth consistency. Return to heat, add salt and let it simmer for about ten minutes.
4. When it is thick, take it off the heat and serve with rice, *kadhi* or *osaman*.

Serves 4-6

OSAMAN
Spiced Split Gram Water

++++++++++++++++++++++++

INGREDIENTS

Yellow split gram	½ cup	Cumin seeds	¼ tsp
Ginger–chilli paste	1 tsp	Asafoetida	¼ tsp
Kokum	4-6 pieces	Curry leaves	a few
Jaggery	3-4 tbsps	Green chilli, slit	1
Turmeric powder	½ tsp	White radish, thinly sliced	2 inch piece
For Tempering		*To Garnish*	
Ghee	1 tbsp	Grated coconut	
Fenugreek seeds	¼ tsp	Coriander leaves	

METHOD

1. Pressure-cook the yellow split gram with eight to nine cups of water. When cool, churn well and add ginger-chilli paste, *kokum*, jaggery and turmeric powder. Boil this for ten to fifteen minutes.
2. Heat *ghee* in a small pan, add fenugreek seeds, mustard and cumin seeds.
3. When they splutter, add asafoetida, curry leaves, green chilli and radish.
4. Pour this tempering over the *osaman*. Simmer it for ten minutes. Garnish with scraped coconut and green coriander leaves.
5. Serve hot at the end of a meal as a digestive or serve with rice and *lachko dal*.

Serves 6

KHATTI-MITTHI DAL

Sweet and Sour Split Gram

++

INGREDIENTS

For the Dal

Red split gram, washed and soaked .... 1 cup
Peanuts 10-12
Ginger-chilli paste .... 1 tsp
Turmeric powder .... ¼ tsp
Kokum .... 3-4 pieces
Jaggery .... 2-3 tbsps
Salt .... to taste

For Tempering

Ghee .... 1 tbsp

Cumin seeds .... ¼ tsp
Fenugreek seeds .... ¼ tsp
Mustard seeds .... ½ tsp
Cinnamon sticks .... 2 pieces
Cloves .... 3-4 pieces
Green chillies 1-2
Curry leaves 6-8
Asafoetida .... a pinch

METHOD

1. Pressure-cook the gram along with peanuts and four to five cups of water. When cool, churn well with the wooden beater. Add all the ingredients for the gram and boil for ten to fifteen minutes.
2. In a small tempering vessel heat *ghee*, add mustard, cumin and fenugreek seeds in it. Let them splutter, add cloves, cinnamon sticks, asafoetida and curry leaves.
3. Pour this over the boiling gram. Boil for five minutes and serve hot with rice.

Serves 4

FAJETO
Mango Flavoured Curry
+++++++++++++++++++++++

INGREDIENTS

Ripe mango .... 1 medium sized	*For Tempering*
Water.................................. 2 cups	*Ghee* .... 1 tbsp
Gram flour ....1 tbsp	Cinnamon sticks and cloves... 3-4 pieces (each)
Sugar ....1 tsp	Curry leaves ....5-6 pieces
Ginger-chilli paste ....1 tsp	Cumin seeds .... ½ tsp
Chilli powder...........................1 tsp	Green chilli, broken .... 1 piece
Salt .... to taste	*To Garnish*
Beaten yogurt ....½ cup	Finely chopped coriander

METHOD

1. Peel and cut the mango. Add half a cup of water and churn in a blender. Pass it through a sieve to get a smooth puree.
2. Add water, gram flour, sugar, ginger-chilli paste, chilli powder and salt. Mix well. Heat *ghee* in a thick saucepan; add all the tempering ingredients and then add the mango juice mixture.
3. Bring to a boil. Simmer for five to ten minutes. Add beaten yogurt and mix well. Garnish with coriander leaves and serve hot with rice.

Serves 4-6

UGELA MUNG
Sprouted Green Grams
+++++++++++++++++++++++++++++++++++++

INGREDIENTS

Whole green gram .... 1 cup	Coriander leaves, finely chopped .... ¼ cup
Oil.. 2 tbsps	Ginger-chilli paste .... 2 tsps
Asafoetida.. ¼ tsp	Turmeric powder .... ¼ tsp
Green chillies, slit 2	Juice of ½ a lemon
Garlic .... 2-3 cloves	Salt .... to taste

METHOD

1. Soak *gram* for eight hours or overnight. Remove water and tie them in a muslin cloth and place in a covered vessel. The gram will sprout well within twelve hours.
2. Heat oil in a saucepan, add asafoetida, green chilli, garlic and coriander leaves. Fry for one minute. Add ginger-chilli paste and cook further for half a minute. Add sprouted gram along with one cup of water and salt. Cover and cook until tender.
3. Add lemon juice. Cook for five more minutes. Serve hot.

Serves 4-6

(See photo on page 17)

KERI NU SHAAK
Sweet and Spicy Mango Pickle
+++++++++++++++++++++++++++++++++++++

INGREDIENTS

Salt .... 1 tsp	*For Tempering*
Turmeric powder................................ ½ tsp	Oil .... 1 tsp
Raw mango, peeled and chopped into ½ inch	Mustard seeds .... ½ tsp
pieces.. 1 cup	Fenugreek seeds .... ½ tsp
Jaggery, chopped............................... 1 cup	Asafoetida .... ½ tsp
Red chilli powder................................ 1 tsp	Round red chillies.............................. 2-3

METHOD

1. Apply salt and turmeric powder to the mango pieces and set aside for half an hour or till the mango begins to leave some water. Drain and take it out in a bowl.
2. Heat oil in a medium sized thick saucepan. Add mustard and fenugreek seeds. When they splutter add asafoetida and chillies along with mango pieces. Keep stirring on low heat. When the mango pieces are slightly soft, add jaggery and keep stirring until the jaggery melts and the gravy is little thick.
3. Remove from heat and add red chilli powder. Set aside to cool. When completely cool and thick fill it up in a jar and store in a cool place.

Makes approx. 250 gms of pickle

KACHA PAPAYA NU SHAAK
Raw Papaya Salad

++

INGREDIENTS

Oil ....1 tbsp	Raw *papaya*, peeled, halved and sliced ....
Mustard seeds .... 1 tsp	.... 250 gms
Asafoetida.............................. a pinch	Coriander leaves, chopped....................1 tbsp
Curry leaves .... a few	Salt ....to taste
Green chillies, slit 3-4	Sugar ....to taste
Ginger, finely chopped .... 1inch piece	Lemon juice ....to taste
Fresh turmeric, peeled and chopped ...... 2 pieces	

METHOD

1. Heat oil in a small saucepan, add mustard seeds to it and when they splutter add asafoetida, curry leaves, chillies, ginger and turmeric powder.
2. Cook for three to four minutes, stirring occasionally. Add raw papaya and let it cook till semi-soft. Add seasonings and mix well.
3. Turn it out on a serving bowl, garnish with coriander and serve at room temperature.

Note :   *You could even grate the papaya instead of slicing it.*

Serves 4

KHAMAN KAKDI
Cucumber and Coconut Salad

++

INGREDIENTS

Cucumber, peeled and chopped or grated	Sugar .... 1 tsp
.... 250 gms	Juice of 1 lemon
Scraped fresh coconut ....3-4 tbsps	Salt .... to taste
Green chillies, deseeded and chopped........... 3-4	**To Garnish**
Peanuts or grams, coarsely ground.........3-4 tbsps	Finely chopped coriander leaves

METHOD

1. Apply salt to the cucumber and set aside for half an hour. Rinse off the excess water from the cucumber and place it in a bowl.
2. Add the rest of the ingredients to the cucumber, garnish and chill until ready to serve.

Serves 4-6

(See photo on page 17)

45

VAGARELI CHAAS
Spiced Buttermilk

+++

INGREDIENTS

Yogurt	1 cup	Coriander leaves finely chopped	1 tbsp
Water	2 cups	Ginger finely chopped	1 tbsp
Oil	1 tsp	Mint leaves finely chopped	1 tbsp
Cumin seeds	¼ tsp	Green chillies finely chopped	1tbsp
Curry leaves	1 tbsp	Salt	to taste

METHOD

1. Beat the yogurt with a whisk. Add water and continue beating till smooth. In a tempering vessel, heat oil and cumin seeds.
2. When they splutter, add curry leaves, coriander, ginger, mint and chillies. Pour this over the beaten yogurt. Add salt to taste. Serve at room temperature or cold.

Makes 4 glasses

(See photo on page 17)

MASALA NI CHAI
Spiced Tea

+++

INGREDIENTS

Milk	1 cup	Cardamoms, freshly crushed in shell	1
Water	1 cup	Tea leaves (strong variety)	2 tsps
Tea *masala* (recipe given below)	1 tsp	A few lemon grass leaves, chopped (optional)	
Sugar	3 tsps		

METHOD

1. In a stainless steel vessel, mix together milk and water, put it to boil on medium heat. Add tea masala, sugar, cardamom and tea leaves. Allow it to boil till the mixture takes a rich golden colour.
2. Add lemon grass, turn the heat off and cover and let it stand for 5 minutes. Strain in individual teacups and serve hot.

<u>*Note :*</u>   *Adjust sugar and tea masala according to your taste.*

Makes 2 cups

<u>*Tea Masala*</u>

Take ten grams each of black pepper, cinnamon, cloves and dried ginger. Add forty grams of whole cardamom. Put all the ingredients in a dry grinder and process till powdered. Store in an airtight jar.

CHHUNDO
Sweet Mango Pickle
++++++++++++++++++++++++++++++

INGREDIENTS

Big sized mangoes (*Rajapuri variety*), peeled and grated (Measure the mango shreds in a cup measure) .... 3 pieces
Rock salt, crushed .... 1/3 cup
Cumin seeds, slightly crushed .... 3 tbsps

Red chilli powder ....2 tbsps
A pinch of asafoetida (*optional*)
Sugar .... 1 ½ times the quantity of mango shreds, coarsely ground

METHOD

1. Mix together grated mango and salt. Set aside for half an hour. Slightly squeeze the mangoes and drain out the excess water. Do this very lightly. In a large vessel mix the grated mango and sugar.
2. Cover and set aside overnight. In the morning remove the lid and tie a muslin cloth on the mouth of the vessel and place it in the sun for three to four days.
3. Stir every evening to mix well. At the end of the fourth day if the syrup has reached a two string consistency that means that the pickle is done but if not then keep it in the sun for one more day. After a two-string syrup has been formed, add cumin seeds, chilli powder and asafoetida.
4. Cover and keep in the shade for one more day. Fill it in a large screw top jar and store in a dry cool place the next day.

Makes 1 ½-2kg

(See photo on page 17)

SUKO SAMBHAR
Spice Mix for Pickles
++++++++++++++++++++++++++++++++++

INGREDIENTS

Split mustard seeds .... 2 cups
Split fenugreek seeds ....1 tbsp
Turmeric powder...¼ cup
Asafoetida.. 4-5 tbsp
Rock salt, slightly crushed .... 2 cups

Red chilli powder (spicy variety) .... 3 cups
Mustard oil, heated and cooled ....2-2½ cups
To Sprinkle
A few black peppercorns

METHOD

1. In a large vessel, mix together split mustard and fenugreek seeds. Add turmeric powder, asafoetida, salt and chilli powder in turn, mixing well after each edition.
2. When you are able to make a dumpling with the spices, this is an indication that it has absorbed enough oil. Fill it in a glass jar and store it in a dry cool place.
3. Use as required for mango pickle, to spice up any food or use it as an accompaniment to your meal.

Makes 7½ cups

GOL KERI
Mango Pickle with Jaggery
+++++++++++++++++++++++++++++++

INGREDIENTS

Raw mangoes, peeled and cut into cubes	Split mustard grains .... 1½ cups
.... 6 large	Split fenugreek grains .... 2 tbsps
Salt .... 3 tbsps	Jaggery, chopped .... 6 cups
Turmeric powder .... 2 tsps	Asafoetida .... 3 tsps
Red chilli powder .... 1 cup	

METHOD

1. Toss mango pieces with salt and turmeric powder. Spread them on a cloth and dry overnight in the shade. Next day mix the remaining spices, chopped jaggery and mango pieces in a large vessel.
2. Toss gently to mix. Fill this in a wide mouthed glass jar and cover the lid with a muslin cloth. Store it in a cupboard in a cool place (not in the kitchen). Stir with a clean spoon once in two days.
3. The pickle is ready when the jaggery has melted and the mango pieces are slightly softened. Take out 250 gms at a time in a small jar for every day use. Enjoy with an Indian meal.

Makes approx. 5 kg

METHIA KERI
Fenugreek Flavoured Mango Pickle
+++++++++++++++++++++++++++++++

INGREDIENTS

Rock salt, slightly crushed .... ¾ cup	Fenugreek seeds .... ¼ cup
Turmeric powder .... 1 tsp	Split fenugreek grains .... 1 cup
Raw mangoes, washed and cut into cubes .... 1 kg	Asafoetida .... 1 tsp
Red chilli powder .... 2 cups	Mustard oil, heated and cooled .... ½-¾-cup
Split mustard grains .... 2 tbsps	

METHOD

1. Apply little salt and turmeric powder to the mango pieces and set aside for one to two hours. Mix all the dry spices together in a bowl. Rub mango pieces with the spice mixture and pile them up in a glass jar. Press them down lightly as you fill the jar.
2. Pour cooled oil from top to cover the surface. Cover the jar tightly and store it in a cool place. Allow the mangoes to marinate for eight to ten days.
3. Stir the pickle from time to time. If it feels a little dry at any point, you may add little extra oil. Fill it in little jars and use as required.

Makes 1½ kg

(See photo on page 18)

MURABBA
Sweet Mango Pickle
+++++++++++++++++++++++++

INGREDIENTS

Mango pieces, peeled and boiled in water .... 4 cups	Cardamom seeds .... 1 tsp
Sugar .... 5 cups	Saffron (powdered) .... 1 tsp

METHOD

1. Mix boiled and drained mango pieces and sugar in a thick vessel and allow it to cook over medium heat. Stir it from time to time.
2. When the syrup becomes one string consistency, remove from fire and add cardamom and saffron. Set aside to cool. Fill in the jar and store in a dry cool place.

Makes 1½ kg

SUTARFENI DELIGHT
Soft Vermicelli Sweet
+++

INGREDIENTS

Cottage cheese grated .... 1 cup	*Sutarfeni*, white or with saffron (purchased) .... 250 gms x 2 circles
Icing sugar, sieved .... ½ cup	Sugar syrup .... ¼ cup
Corn flour .... 1 tsp	
Fruit of your choice, freshly chopped (Pineapple, orange, mango, chopped mixed dry fruits) .... ½ cup	**To Garnish** A few rose petals and relevant fruits sliced

METHOD

1. In a medium bowl place cottage cheese, icing sugar and corn flour and mix well. Add finely chopped fruit of your choice to this mixture. Now place one of the *sutarfeni* onto a lightly greased baking tray and slightly heat in a moderate oven, just to make it a little crisp.
2. Remove from oven and let it cool slightly. Place *sutarfeni* onto a serving dish and spread cottage cheese mixture over this evenly. Make the other *sutarfeni* slightly crisp in oven and place that over the cottage cheese mixture.
3. Pour sugar syrup over the *sutarfeni*, make sure it does not leak out from the sides. Decorate with rose petals and the fruit slices. Cut it into triangle pieces and serve at room temperature or cold.

Serves 6-8

JALEBI
Pretzel Shaped Sweet
+++++++++++++++++++++++++

INGREDIENTS

Plain flour (*maida*)	2 cups	Saffron (powdered)	1 tsp
Plain yogurt	1 ½ cups	Ghee	for frying
Warm water	½ cup	**To Garnish**	
Hot *ghee*	3 tbsps	Almonds and pistachios, sliced	3-4 tbsps
Sugar	½ kg	A few rose petals	
Cardamom powder	1 tsp		

METHOD

1. Soak flour in yogurt, warm water and three tablespoons of hot *ghee*. Beat this mixture vigorously so that it becomes lump free. Cover and keep this vessel in a warm place. If the weather is cold you need to do this two nights before.
2. Make one string syrup from sugar using just enough water. Add cardamom and saffron powder to it and keep it warm on a slow fire. When you want to serve, heat *ghee* for frying in a broad vessel. Beat the *jalebi* mixture to a dropping consistency.
3. Fill a cylindrical bottle with a small spout with this mixture. Form spiral shaped rounds over hot *ghee* not too close to each other.
4. Turn them over time to time with the help of a pair of tongs. When they are golden coloured, remove them and soak them in hot syrup which you keep by the side.
5. Let it soak for five to seven minutes and remove on a serving plate. Garnish with almonds, pistachios and rose petals and serve at once. Make the rest of the portions as required.

Serves 6-8

(See photo on page 18)

SHRIKHAND
Saffron Flavoured Yogurt
+++++++++++++++++++++++++++

INGREDIENTS

Plain yogurt	250 gms	Cardamom powder	½ tsp
Sugar	3-4 tbsps	**To Garnish**	
Saffron	a few strands	Thinly sliced almonds and pistachios	

METHOD

1. Tie yogurt in a muslin cloth for an hour or till all the water is drained out. Place it in a bowl and mix sugar. Put it through a sieve to get a smooth consistency.
2. Mix saffron threads in a little water and add this to the yogurt along with cardamom powder.
3. Mix well and transfer to a serving bowl. Sprinkle the nuts and refrigerate until ready to serve.

Serves 2

BADAM KATLI
Diamond Shaped Almond Sweet

+++++++++++++++++++++++++++++++

INGREDIENTS

Almonds	2 cups	Saffron	a few strands
Sugar	¾ cup	Thin silver foil sheets	2-3
Cardamom powder	½ tsp	*Ghee*	1 tbsp

METHOD

1. Drop almonds in hot water and let them stand for ten minutes. Remove from water and peel off the skin. Pat dry them. Grind it to a fine powder.

2. Place sugar in a thick vessel and add enough water to cover the surface. Put it on high flame to make the syrup. Boil it till it forms two to three strings. Add cardamom powder and saffron, mixing it with a little water. Add almond powder and continue mixing.

3. When the sugar and almond have mixed properly, remove from heat (approx. two to three minutes). Apply *ghee* on the counter or the work surface. Pour the mixture on it. Start rolling to get the required thickness.

4. Even out the mixture and press silver foil to cover. Cut diagonally to make diamond shapes. Let it cool to room temperature. Remove with sharp, flat spoon. Store it in an airtight box.

Makes 24 pieces

KHOPRA PAK
Coconut Sweet
+++++++++++++++++++++++++++++++

INGREDIENTS

Freshly scraped coconut .... 5 cups
Fresh cream from the top of the milk......... ½ cup
Ghee .... 1 tbsp
Sugar .... 1 ½ cup
Condensed milk .... 1 cup
Saffron powder .... ½ tsp
Cardamom powder .... 1 tsp
Pistachios, chopped into pieces .... 2 tbsps

METHOD

1. In a large vessel, mix together coconut and cream and set aside for half an hour. Apply *ghee* to a fourteen inch stainless steel or a silver plate with a high rim and set aside. Heat a broad thick vessel (*kadai*), add the soaked coconut and dry roast it for 8-10 minutes.

2. When the coconut looks a little dry, add sugar and condensed milk and mix well. Cook on medium heat for fifteen to twenty minutes. Check with your finger if it has formed a thick syrup of one strand and then remove from heat.

3. Add powdered saffron mixed with a little milk and cardamom powder in it. Mix well, pour this into the prepared stainless steel plate and smoothen the surface with the back of a spoon. Sprinkle pistachio pieces on the top.

4. Let it cool completely. Cut across to make one inch by one inch square or diamond pieces. Take it out of the plate with the help of a flat spoon and put it on a serving plate.

5. Garnish with rose petals.

Makes approx. 34 pieces

MANGO PARFAIT

++++++++++++++++++++++++++++++++++++

INGREDIENTS

Milk .... 2 cups

Sugar .... ½ cup

Corn flour .... 2 tbsps

Gelatine, mixed with ¼ cup of water .... 1½ tbsps

Lemon juice .... ½ tsp

Mango pulp .... ½ cup

Alphonso mangoes, peeled and chopped ....
.... 2 medium sized

Fresh cream, beaten .... ¾ cup

To Garnish

A few chopped mango pieces

METHOD

1. In a medium saucepan, mix together milk, sugar and corn flour. Bring to a boil stirring all the time. Simmer and cook until thick. Remove from heat and set aside to cool.
2. In a small pan, heat the gelatine mixture until dissolved. Add lemon juice and cool. Beat this into the cooled milk along with the cream.
3. Divide this mixture into two parts. Add mango pulp to one part and half of the chopped mangoes to the other.
4. Take individual stemmed glasses and layer both the custards alternatively with mango pieces in between. The top layer should be of the chopped mangoes.
5. Chill in the Refrigerator for one to two hours before serving.

Serves 6

SPICY MISAL
Spicy Sprouts Mixture
+++++++++++++++++++++++++++++++

INGREDIENTS

For the Misal
Small variety *matki*, soaked and sprouted............
.... 1 cup
Medium potatoes, boiled and cut into small
pieces..2
Black *masala* .... ½ tsp
Garam masala .... ½ tsp
Chilli powder...1 tsp
Crushed garlic and ginger .... 2 tsps
Lemon juice .... 2 tsps

Oil ....3 tbsps
Water .... 4 cups
Salt .... to taste
To Serve
Poha chivda .... 1 cup
Indian savoury mixture............................1 cup
Onion, finely chopped ....1 cup
Coriander, finely chopped ....2 tbsps
Lemon, cut into bits 1
Sour dough bread(*pav*) 4-6

METHOD

FOR THE MISAL

1. Wash, drain and boil the *matki* until tender. Do not allow the seeds to burst. Drain and keep aside. In one cup of water make a paste of all the *masalas*.
2. Heat the oil in a large deep saucepan and add ginger-garlic paste. Stir-fry for one minute. Add the *masala* mixture and the potatoes.
3. Mix well. Stir-fry until the oil separates. Add the boiled *matki* and the remaining one cup of water. Allow it to boil. Simmer on a low flame for ten to fifteen minutes. Add salt, lemon juice and keep hot.

TO SERVE

In an individual serving bowl, place one tablespoon of *chivda* at the bottom and put the *farsaan* over it. Pour a ladle full of *misal* over this. Garnish with chopped onions and coriander. Squeeze lemon over it and serve with *pav*.

Serve 4-6

Spicy Misal

PITLA AND BHAKRI

Gram Flour Curry with Millet Bread
One of the Favourite Meals of Maharashtrian Farmers

+++

INGREDIENTS

For the Pitla
Gram flour .... 1 cup
Turmeric powder .... ¼ tsp
Lemon juice .... 1 tsp
Salt .... to taste
Water + Buttermilk .... 2-2 ½ cups
Spring onions, finely chopped 2
Green chillies, slit 4-5
Curry leaves 3-4
Garlic .... 1 tsp
Oil... 3 tbsps

Mustard .... ½ tsp
Cumin seeds .... ½ tsp
Asafoetida .... ½ tsp
For the Bhakri
Millet flour .... 2 cups
Yogurt... 2 tbsps
Salt .... to taste
Water to bind the dough
To Serve
White butter
Chilli-garlic *thecha*

METHOD

FOR THE PITLA

1. Make a smooth paste of gram flour, turmeric powder, lemon, salt, and water. Mix in ginger, garlic, onion and green chillies. Set aside.
2. Heat oil in a wide pan, add mustard and cumin seeds and allow it to splutter. Then add asafoetida, curry leaves and fry for two minutes. Add the batter. Stir while adding. Keep stirring until all the lumps have broken and it begins to boil.
3. Adjust the seasoning. Cook on a slow flame for six to seven minutes. Serve hot with *bhakri*.

FOR THE BHAKRI

1. Add salt to the flour. Make a soft dough by adding yogurt and water. Take a lump of the dough, dust it with flour and pat it with your palm to flatten it out.
2. Use the rotary motion to make a round flat bread (could be thick or thin, as you desire). Place this carefully on a griddle, flip and roast both sides completely.
3. Then put on a direct flame for a few seconds and make it as crisp as you like it. Serve hot with *pitla*, chilli-garlic *thecha* and white butter.

CHILLI-GARLIC THECHA

Coarsely pound in a mortar ten to twelve green chillies, six to eight cloves garlic, one teaspoon of salt and one teaspoon of *ghee*.

Serves 4-6

BHARLI VANGI
Stuffed Aubergine
+++++++++++++++++++++++++++++++++++

INGREDIENTS

Oil	5 tbsps	Small round brinjals, stem trimmed, and slit length into 4	8-10
Peppercorns	6	Potatoes, peeled and quartered	3
Cloves	6	Chilli powder	1 tsp
Coriander leaves, chopped	1 cup	Coriander seeds	1 ½ tbsps
Onions, sliced	3	Black *masala*	1 tsp
Coconut, grated	1 cup	Turmeric powder	½ tsp
Tamarind pulp	1 tsp	**To Garnish**	
Cashew nuts, finely chopped	20 pieces	Finely chopped coriander leaves	
Sugar	1 tsp		
Salt	to taste		

METHOD

1. Heat one tablespoon of oil in a thick vessel and add peppercorns, cloves, coriander seeds, sliced onion and coconut. Roast till brown and grind to a fine paste with water.
2. To this paste add all powders, tamarind pulp, cashews, sugar and salt. Stuff this mixture into the slits in *brinjals* and mix the potatoes with the remaining mixture.
3. Heat the remaining oil is a pressure pan. Arrange brinjals and potato mixture around. Add one cup of water and cook under pressure for five to seven minutes. Transfer to a serving bowl. Garnish with coriander leaves and serve hot with *bhakris*.

Serves 4-6

(See photo on page 56)

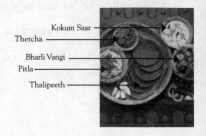

Kokum Saar
Thetcha
Bharli Vangi
Pitla
Thalipeeth

AMSULA CHE SAAR
Kokum Extract
++

INGREDIENTS

Black *Kokums*	6-8	Garlic (optional)	1 clove
Water	1/3 cup	Curry leaves	5-6
Coconut	1 medium	Coriander, finely chopped	2 tbsps
Ghee	2 tbsps	Salt	to taste
Cumin seeds	1 tsp	Sugar	2 tsps
Green chillies, slit and halved	2		

METHOD

1. Wash and soak *kokums* in one-third cup of water for ten minutes. Soak coconut in one cup of water for half an hour. Extract milk by liquidising and straining.

2. Heat *ghee* in a saucepan, add cumin seeds, chillies, garlic (optional), curry leaves. When the seeds splutter, add coconut milk, coriander, salt, sugar and one cup of water.

3. Very gently bring the mixture to luke warm temperature. Discard the *kokums* before serving. You may also serve this at room temperature with rice, or as a drink during a meal.

Serves 4-6

(See photo on page 56)

VAALA CHE BIRDE
Field Beans in Gravy

++

INGREDIENTS

Oil	3-4 tbsps	Soda-bi-carbonate	¼ tsp
Garlic, crushed	2-3 cloves	Salt	to taste
Green chillies, chopped	2-3 pieces	Sugar	1 tsp
Curry leaves	a few	Juice of ½ a lemon	
Field beans, soaked and sprouted	250 gms	**To Garnish**	
Turmeric powder	¼ tsp	Finely chopped coriander and scraped coconut	

METHOD

1. Heat three tablespoons of oil in a saucepan, fry garlic, green chillies and curry leaves for one minute. Add sprouted beans and mix well so that the oil is coated to the beans.
2. Mix half a cup of water with one tablespoon of oil, turmeric powder and soda-bi-carbonate. Add this to the field beans. Cook on a medium flame until soft. Add salt, sugar and lemon juice.
3. Garnish with coriander and coconut and serve hot.

Serves 4

AMBTI
Spicy and Sour Gravy

+++++++++++++++++++++++

INGREDIENTS

Oil	2 tbsps	Tamarind pulp	1 tbsp
Asafoetida	¼ tsp	Salt	to taste
Garlic, crushed	4-5 cloves	Yellow split gram cooked in 6-7 cups water and drained	1 cup
Curry leaves	a few		
Red chilli powder	1 ½ tsp	Cumin seeds	1 tsp
Black *masala*	2 tsps	**To Garnish**	
Red split gram water (from the *puran*)	4-5 cups	Finely chopped coriander	
Jaggery	2 tbsps	Scraped coconut	

METHOD

1. Heat oil in a saucepan. Add cumin seeds, asafoetida, garlic and curry leaves. Add chilli powder and black *masala* and roast for two to three minutes.
2. Add gram *water* and boil it on low heat. Add jaggery, tamarind and salt. Boil till all the spices are mixed well.
3. Garnish with coconut and coriander and serve hot with *puran poli* or rice.

Makes 7-8 servings

PURAN POLI
Sweet Stuffed Bread
++++++++++++++++++++++++++++

INGREDIENTS

Bengal gram	1 cup	Wheat flour	½ cup
Jaggery	1 cup	Rice flour	½ cu
Nutmeg, grated	½	Salt	½ tsp
Cardamoms, seeds removed and powdered		Oil	¼ cup
	8-10	*To Serve*	
A few threads of saffron		Ghee	15 tsps

METHOD

1. Boil gram in four to six cups of water. Cook until grams are soft. While it is hot, drain all the water out and keep aside to make the *ambti*. While the gram is hot, add jaggery and cook until both are incorporated. Set aside to cool.
2. Make the mixture into a thick paste by grinding it on a stone or using the blender. Add nutmeg, cardamom and saffron. Now divide this mixture into fifteen walnut sized balls. Make the dough with both wheat snd rice flours, salt and oil.
3. Divide this into fifteen round parts, the shape slightly larger than the walnut. Place one of the jaggery-gram ball in the centre of each ball and close it like a round dumpling.
4. Press this between your palms to a flat disc. Now roll it out to rounds of eight to nine inches. Dry roast it on a hot griddle, turning on both sides. Serve hot with one teaspoon of *ghee* on each *poli*.

Makes 15 puran polies

BHAKHARVADI
Rolled Potato Snack
++++++++++++++++++++++++++++++++++

INGREDIENTS

For the **Dough**

Plain flour ....500 gms

Gram flour ....100 gms

Salt .... to taste

Oil...¼ cup

For the **Filling**

Potatoes, boiled and mashed..................500 gms

Garam masala .... 1 tbsp

Fresh coriander, chopped ....3 tbsps

Ginger-chilli paste .... 1 tbsp

Chilli powder .... 1 tsp

Dry coconut, grated ....2 tbsps

Sesame seeds, toasted ....2 tbsps

Gramflour vermicelli (*Sev*) .... 100 gms

Juice of ½ a lemon

METHOD

1. Mix together both the flours and salt. Add in the oil and then add enough water to form a semi-soft dough and divide it into three portions. Set aside. Mix all the ingredients or the filling and divide into three parts.
2. Roll out one part of the dough into one big *roti*, spread the mixture evenly all over the surface and roll it tightly. Cut into one inch pieces.
3. Set aside for half an hour and fry them in hot oil until crisp and golden. Drain and serve hot.

Makes 20-24 pieces

THALI PEETH
Mixed Flour Bread
+++++++++++++++++++++++++++++++++++

INGREDIENTS

Thali peeth flour (recipes follows)	1 cup	Oil for frying	1 + 4 tbsps
Green chilli, chopped	1 tbsp	Sesame seeds, toasted	1 tbsp
Ginger, chopped	1 tbsp	Clove-cardamom powder	½ tsp
Onion, finely chopped	1	Coriander-cumin powder	½ tsp
Red chilli powder	1 tsp	Pepper	¼ tsp
Sour yogurt	½ cup	Salt	to taste
Tomato, finely chopped	1		

METHOD

1. Place flour in a broad dish. Add all ingredients except oil to make a soft dough. Heat a griddle with one tablespoon of oil.
2. Make small balls of the dough. Place them on a rolling board and press lightly with your palm to make small rounds of approximately three inch in diameter.
3. Place the *thali peeth* on hot griddle. Apply a little oil on the top surface, cover the pan and let it cook on a slow flame. Turn it over and cook the other side.
4. When it is light brown, take it off the gas and serve with vegetables or *pitla*.

Make approx. 12 pieces

Thali Peeth flour

Raw rice	1 cup	Cumin seeds	½ tsp
Wheat	¼ cup	Whole black pepper	½ tsp
Dark millet (*Bajri*)	¼ cup	Fenugreek seeds	½ tsp
White millet (*Jawar*)	¼ cup	Clove powder	½ tsp
Bengal gram	¼ cup	Cardemom powder	½ tsp
Coriander seeds	½ tsp		

Roast and dry grind all the ingredients and fill in an airtight jar. Use as required.

Makes 4 cups

MASALA CHE BHAAT
Spicy Rice

++

INGREDIENTS

Ghee .... 4-5 tbsps	Fresh coconut, chopped .... 2 tbsps
Asafoetida .... ¼ tsp	Lemon juice .... 1 tsp
Mustard seeds .... 1 tsp	Ginger juice .... 1 tsp
Green chillies 2	Water .... 3 cups
Cinnamon .... 2-3 pieces	Turmeric powder .... ½ tsp
Cloves .... 2-3 pieces	Black *masala* .... 2 tsps
Onion, chopped long .... 1 medium sized	*Garam masala* .... 2 tsps
Green peas, shelled .... ½ cup	Chilli powder .... 1 tsp
Tendlies, cut into 4 pieces vertically 10-12	Curry leaves .... a few
Rice, washed, soaked in water for 10 minutes	**To Garnish**
and drained .... 1 ½ cups	Freshly chopped coriander leaves .... ¼ cup
Cashew nuts, chopped .... 2 tbsps	

METHOD

1. Heat *ghee* in a thick vessel and add asafoetida and mustard seeds to it. When they splutter, add green chillies, cinnamon, cloves and turmeric powder.

2. Add onions, green peas and *tendli*. Cook for two to three minutes and add the rice and all the dry spices. Stir and add water.

3. Cover and cook on a slow flame for fifteen minutes, stirring occasionally. Add salt, cashews, coconut pieces and lemon and ginger juice.

4. When rice is soft and cooked, remove from heat and garnish with coriander leaves and serve hot with yogurt.

Note: *You could change the vegetables as per your liking. You can use cauliflower, French beans, brinjal, etc.*

Serves 4-6

64

PATAL BHAJI
Green Leafy Vegetable
+++++++++++++++++++++++++++++++++++

INGREDIENTS

Colacassia leaves with stems	10 stems	Curry leaves	a few
Small bunch of *ambat bhaji* (sour greens)	1	Cinnamon-clove powder	¼ tsp
Peanuts	1 tbsp	*Garam masala*	½ tsp
Bengal Gram	1 tbsp	Black *masala*	2 tsps
Gram flour	2 tbsps	Salt	to taste
Oil	2 tbsps	Sugar	1 tsp
Cumin seeds	½ tsp	Lemon juice	2 tsps
Bay leaf	1	Green chillies	3
Cardamoms	2	Water	5 cups

METHOD

1. Chop both greens coarsely with stems. Wash, drain and place them in a pressure cooker in one container with half a cup of water. In the other container place grams and peanuts with half a cup of water.
2. Give the cooker four whistles. Cool, remove and blend the greens with a hand mixer. Add gram flour to half a cup of water. Make it a smooth paste and set aside.
3. Heat oil, add cumin seeds, bay leaf, cardamoms, curry leaves and cinnamon-clove powder. Stir for a few minutes.
4. Add boiled peanuts and grams with the water. Bring to a boil. Add blended greens, *masalas*, salt, sugar and lemon. Add the remaining water and stir well.
5. Bring to boil and add gram flour paste, stirring continuously. Simmer for five to seven minutes. Serve hot with rice or *bhakri*.

Serves 4-6

KANDE-BATATE CHI BHAAJI
Onion-Potato Vegetable

++

INGREDIENTS

Oil	4-5 tbsps	Salt	to taste
Cumin seeds	1 tsp	Dry coconut, grated	3-4 tbsps
Asafoetida	½ tsp	Jaggery, chopped	1 tbsp
Onions, peeled and cut long	250 gms	Tamarind pulp	1 tbsp
Potatoes, peeled and cut long	250 gms	**To Garnish**	
Black *masala*	2 tbsps	Finely chopped coriander	
Chilli powder	1 tsp		

METHOD

1. Heat oil in a thick and broad vessel, add cumin seeds and asafoetida. When seeds begin to splutter, add onions and fry for two minutes.
2. Add potatoes, black *masala*, chilli powder and salt. Cover the vessel with water on top and cook vegetables on low heat. Stir from time to time.
3. When vegetables are soft, add dry coconut, jaggery and tamarind pulp. Cook further for five minutes. Garnish with coriander and serve hot with *bhakri*.

Serves 4-6

PANCHAMRUT
Yogurt with Five Ingredients

++++++++++++++++++++++++++++++++++

INGREDIENTS

Finely chopped cucumber	¼ cup	Fresh green chilli, chopped	1
Tomatoes	¼ cup	Mint, finely chopped	1 tbsp
Onion	¼ cup	Coriander leaves, finely chopped	1 tbsp
Carrots	¼ cup	Roasted and powdered cumin seeds	½ tsp
Ground peanuts	¼ cup	Salt	to taste
Thick yogurt	1½-2 cups	Sugar	to taste

METHOD

1. Mix all ingredients together in a bowl and mix well.
2. Chill until ready to serve.

Makes 3 cups

GARLIC CHUTNEY

++++++++++++++++++++++++++++++++++++

INGREDIENTS

Dry red chillies (*bedki* variety)	50	Cumin seeds	1 tsp
Garlic cloves	½ cup	Enough oil to bind it	
Salt	3 tsps		

METHOD

1. Soak the chillies for fifteen minutes in water and remove.
2. Clean the garlic and make a paste on the stone with the help of a mortar.
3. Add salt and cumin seeds.
4. Make a fine paste with the help of a little oil.
5. Store it in an airtight bottle.

Makes ½ cup

BLACK MASALA

++++++++++++++++++++++++++++++++++++

INGREDIENTS

Dry coconut, grated	1 ¼ cup	Cinnamon	8-10 pieces
Coriander seeds	5 cups	Cardamoms	15
Sesame seeds	¼ cup	Mace	2 tbsps
Cumin seeds	¼ cup	Asafoetida	4 tsp s
Caraway seeds	¼ cup	Turmeric powder	2 tbsps
Poppy seeds	¾ cup	Red chilli powder	¾ cup
Mustard seeds	2 tsps	Salt	¼ cup
Fenugreek seeds	1 tsp	Bay leaves	10-12
Cloves	4 tsps	Oil	for roast

METHOD

1. Roast the coconut in a little oil until light brown and set aside.
2. Sauté the coriander seeds, sesame seeds, cumin seeds, caraway seeds and poppy seeds in a little oil and keep aside.
3. Sauté mustard seeds and fenugreek seeds in a little oil. Add cloves and cinnamon. Remove cardamom seeds.
4. Make a powder out of all the sautéed spices, mace and coconut.
5. Mix this powder with asafoetida, turmeric powder, red chilli powder and salt. Store in an airtight bottle.

Makes 1 ½ kg

67

SABUDANA VADA
Sago-Potato Dumpling

++++++++++++++++++++++++++++++++++++

INGREDIENTS

Potatoes, boiled and mashed	500 gms	Salt	to taste
Dried sago	½ cup	Sugar	1 tsp
Ginger-chilli paste	2 tbsps	Arrowroot	1 tbsp
Powder peanuts	½ cup	Oil	for frying
Finely chopped coriander	¼ cup	Soaked sago	2 tbsps
Grated fresh coconut	2 tbsps	*To Serve*	
Juice of 1 lemon		Green *chutney* (Recipe on page 19)	

METHOD

1. Soak sago in one cup of water. Drain and set aside.
2. Mix all the ingredients except oil in a bowl. Make walnut sized balls from this mixture.
3. Roll these balls in soaked sago and fry in hot oil.
4. Serve as a snack with green *chutney*.

Serves 6-8

PUNJABI CHOLE
Chickpeas in Black Spice
+++

INGREDIENTS

Chickpeas, soaked overnight	500 gms	Nigella seeds	3 tsps
Tea bags	2	Pomegranate seeds	3 tsps
Turmeric	½ tsp	Coriander seeds	2 tbsps
Salt	½ tsp	Black cumin seeds	2 tbsps
Oil	4 tbsps	*Garam masala*	1 tbsp
Ginger-chilli paste	4 tbsps	Seeds of big cardamom	1 tbsp
Gram flour	2 tbsps	Bay leaves	3-4
Tamarind water	2 tbsps	Black peppercorns	8-10
Onions, grated	250 gms		
Potatoes, boiled, peeled and cubed	250 gms		
Tomatoes, grated	4		

To Garnish

Rock salt, sliced onions, thinly sliced ginger, coriander leaves and slit green chillies

To be Powdered

Chilli powder .... 3 tsps

METHOD

1. Pressure cook the chick peas with the water they were soaked in with half a teaspoon of turmeric and half a teaspoon of salt. Make strong tea with two tea bags and one cup of water.
2. Add this to the chickpeas and cook until soft. In an iron griddle roast all the ingredients to be powdered with a little oil until brown. Cool the spices and powder it finely. In a heavy saucepan or *kadai*, heat four tablespoons of oil.
3. When the oil is very hot, add the powdered spices and fry for one minute. Then add the gram flour and roast until dark brown. Add onions, ginger-chilli paste and the tomatoes and fry for three to four minutes.
4. Add the cooked chickpeas along with a little water, tamarind water and potatoes. Mix well. Add a little extra water if required and mix well until the spices, chickpeas and water are incorporated properly.
5. Garnish with a little rock salt, ginger, chillies, coriander leaves, and sliced onions. Serve hot with *naan* or *bhatura*.

Serves 6

TADKA DAL
Tempered Yellow Split Gram
+++++++++++++++++++++++++++++

INGREDIENTS

Yellow split gram .... 1 cup
Water .... 4 cups
Turmeric .... ¼ tsp
Ginger .... 1inch piece
For Tempering
Ghee .... 2 tbsps
Cumin seeds .... ½ tsp
Mustard .... ½ tsp

Dry red chillies 3-4
Curry leaves .... a few
Garlic, crushed .... 5-6 cloves
Onion, finely chopped .... 1 medium
Salt .... to taste
To Garnish
Freshly chopped coriander leaves and lemon pieces

METHOD

1. Cook lentils in the pressure cooker with water, turmeric and ginger. Give the cooker three whistles. Let it cool and churn the lentils with a wooden whisk to make it smooth.

2. Set aside. Heat *ghee* in a medium sized saucepan, add cumin and mustard seeds and when they splutter add chillies, curry leaves, garlic and onion. Cook until onions are soft. Remove the ginger piece from the lentils and add them to the saucepan with tempering.

3. Add salt and mix well. Bring to a boil. Garnish with coriander leaves. Serve hot with rice.

Serves 4

PHIRNI
Milk and Almond Pudding
++++++++++++++++++++++++++++

INGREDIENTS

Almonds, soaked over night and blanched .... 12 pieces	Saffron ....a few strands
	To Garnish
Rice, soaked overnight .... 2 tbsps	A pinch of cardamom powder
Milk .... 1 litre	Sliced and toasted, pistachios and almonds and
Sugar .... 1 cup	*varakh*

METHOD

1. Grind almonds and rice separately with little water. Boil milk on moderate heat for thirty minutes, stirring occasionally. Stir in the ground rice and almonds along with the sugar.
2. Continue boiling for ten to fifteen minutes, until the pudding is thick enough to coat the spoon heavily. Remove from heat and add the saffron mixed with little milk.
3. Cool at room temperature. Pour it in an earthen pot and garnish with cardamom powder, chopped nuts and *varakh*.
4. Chill for four hours, until it is thoroughly chilled and firm to touch.

Serves 4-6

(See photo on page 73)

VEGETABLE BIRYANI
Layered Rice with Vegetables

+++

INGREDIENTS

Uncooked *Basmati* rice, washed and soaked .... 2 cups

Mixed vegetables, cubed and boiled (French beans, carrots, potatoes, peas) .... 3 cups

Ghee .... ¼ cup+ 1 tbsp

Onions, sliced and fried .... 4 medium

Tomatoes, liquidized and sieved .... 2½ cups

Turmeric powder................................... ½ tsp

For the Paste

Kashmiri red chillies 10-12

Onions, grated.......................... 4 medium

Coriander powder........................... 1 tbsp

Cumin powder .... 1 tbsp

Khus-khus .... 1 tbsp

Grated dry coconut .... ½ cup

Garlic, peeled .... 2 bulbs

Ginger .... 2 inch piece

Bay leaves .... 2 inch piece

Cinnamon stick .... 2 inch piece

Cloves ....4 pieces

Cardamoms ....4 pieces

Oil to roast .... 2 tbsps

To Garnish

Sliced and Fried Onions

To Serve

Plain yogurt

METHOD

1. Cook one cup of rice with two and one-fourth cup of water with little salt and cook the other cup of rice with two and one-fourth cup of water, salt and turmeric. Set aside to cool.
2. Roast all the ingredients for the paste in oil till it emits a fragrant aroma, cool and make a paste with little water. Heat one-fourth cup of *ghee* in a wide pan; fry the paste till the *ghee* separates. Add tomatoes, vegetables and salt.
3. Cook till the mixture is dry. Set aside to cool. Grease a flat metal or glass dish with one tablespoon of *ghee*. Spread the yellow rice at the bottom.
4. Even out the surface and top it up with the vegetable mixture and a layer of white rice. Press gently again to even out the surface. Cover and set aside till ready to serve.
5. Place the dish in a preheated oven for ten to fifteen minutes before serving. Remove and invert on a serving plate.
6. Garnish with fried onions and serve hot with yogurt.

Serves 8-10

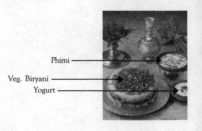

Phirni

Veg. Biryani

Yogurt

DAL MAKHANI
Black Lentils Simmered in Butter

+++++++++++++++++++++++++++++++

INGREDIENTS

Black lentils (soaked overnight) .... 250 gms	Finely chopped ginger .... 2 tbsps
Kidney Beans (soaked overnight) .... 4 tbsps	Finely chopped garlic .... 2 tbsps
Water .... 3 cups	Onions, finely chopped .... 1 cup
Salt .... 1 tsp	*Garam masala* .... 2 tbsps
Ghee .... 3 tbsps	Chopped tomatoes .... 1 cup
Butter .... 3 tbsps	***To Garnish***
Cumin seeds .... 1 tsp	Fresh cream .... 2 tbsps
Chilli powder .... 1 tsp	Fresh coriander leaves, chopped .... 1 tbsp

METHOD

1. Pressure cook lentil with salt, chilli powder, *ghee* and one tablespoon of ginger. Give the cooker three to four whistles.

2. Set aside to cool. Open the cooker and churn *dal* with a wooden whisk until smooth. Add a little warm water if needed. In a heavy saucepan, heat butter; fry cumin seeds, one tablespoon of ginger and garlic for a minute.

3. Add finely chopped onions and fry for seven to eight minutes or until onions are golden brown. Add *garam masala* and tomato and fry for two minutes. Add cooked lentils and simmer for ten minutes, till the mixture is smooth.

4. Garnish with cream and coriander leaves. Serve hot with *naan* or rice.

Serves 6

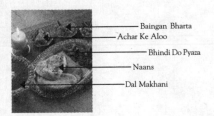

— Baingan Bharta
— Achar Ke Aloo
— Bhindi Do Pyaza
— Naans
— Dal Makhani

MULI PARATHA
White Raddish Bread

++++++++++++++++++++++++++++++++++++

INGREDIENTS

For the Filling
Oil .... 1 tbsp
White radish with leaves, washed and grated .....
.... 2-3 stems (2 cups)
Green chillies chopped .... 3-4 pieces
Dry mango powder .... 1 tsp
Red chilli powder .... 1 tsp
Finely chopped coriander .... 2 tbsps

Turmeric powder .... a pinch
Salt .... to taste
For the Dough
Wheat flour 1½-cup
Plain flour .... ¾ cup
Ghee .... 4 tbsps
Salt .... to taste
Oil .... for frying

METHOD

FOR THE FILLING

Heat oil and cook the radish and chillies for three to four minutes. Remove from heat and add the remaining ingredients. Mix well.

FOR THE DOUGH

1. Make soft dough with wheat flour, plain flour, *ghee* and salt. Divide the dough in twelve to fourteen equal parts.
2. Roll out each one to two inch disc. Place two tablespoons of the radish mixture in the centre and form a small ball. Press it down and roll again to four inch round *paratha*.
3. Roast them on a hot griddle with oil. Serve hot with yogurt or green *chutney*.

Variation: In place of radish you can use spring onions or mint leaves.

Makes 12-14 parathas

CORN AND PANEER PARATHA
Corn-Cottage Cheese Stuffed Bread

++

INGREDIENTS

Corn kernels	1 cup	Sugar	½ tsp
Crumbled cottage cheese	1 cup	Chilli powder	½ tsp
Cream of wheat, roasted	500 gms	*Garam masala*	½ tsp
Ginger-chilli paste	1 tbsp	Salt	to taste
Coriander leaves	1 tbsp	Wheat flour	to roll
Sour yogurt	¼ cup	Oil	for frying
Asafoetida	½ tsp		

METHOD

1. Crush corn kernels and mix it with cottage cheese, cream of wheat, ginger-chilli paste, coriander, curd, asafoetida, sugar, chilli powder, *garam masala* and salt.
2. Add enough wheat flour to make the dough stiff.
3. Divide the dough into walnut sized balls and lightly roll it on the floured surface.
4. Heat little oil on a griddle and fry the *parathas*. Serve hot with garlic *chutney*.

Serves 8

MAKAI KI ROTI
Maize Flour Bread

++

INGREDIENTS

Maize flour	250 gms	Green chillies, finely chopped	2 (small)
Oil	1 tbsp	**To Serve**	
Finely chopped coriander leaves	2 tbsps	White butter	
Salt	½ tsp		

METHOD

1. Mix together flour and salt. Rub in oil, and let it rest for five to ten minutes. Add remaining ingredients and make a soft dough with warm water.
2. Cover and set aside for half an hour. Divide the dough into twelve to fifteen round balls. Roast them on a griddle, greased with a little oil.
3. Continue flattening by pressing all around. Cook on both sides till golden. Smear with a little butter and serve with *sarson ka sag*.

Makes 12-15 rotis

77

NAAN
Puffed Bread
+++++++++++++++++

INGREDIENTS

Plain flour or... 2 cups	Yogurt.. ½ cup
Plain flour mixed with one cup of wheat flour	Milk .... ¼ cup
.... 1 cup	Salt .... to taste
Dried yeast... 2 tsps	**For the Topping** (optional)
Tepid water ....¼ cup	Chopped garlic mixed with 1 tbsp of butter ......
Sugar .... 1 tsp	.... 1 tbsp
Melted *ghee* .... 1 tbsp	Nigella seeds mixed with 1 tbsp of butter .. 1 tsp
....	Poppy seeds mixed with 1 tbsp of butter .... 1 tsp

METHOD

1. Sieve the flour with salt and place it in a large bowl with a well in the centre and set aside. Mix together lukewarm water with dried yeast and sugar in a small bowl and keep it covered in a warm place for ten minutes.

2. When it turns frothy, add it to the flour, along with the *ghee*. Rub this to the flour with your fingertips and make a soft dough with yogurt and milk and keep it covered for two hours or until it doubles in volume.

3. Punch the dough down with your fist and knead it. Divide into eight parts. Roll out each part into a teardrop shaped leaf wide at the base.

4. Bake it either on a greased tray in a hot oven or on a Barbecue grill for about five to six minutes. Garnish it with whatever topping you like and serve hot.

Makes 8 Naans

(See photo on page 74)

MASALA KULCHA
Stuffed Crisp Bread

++

INGREDIENTS

For the Stuffing
Mashed potatoes .... 2½ cups
Grated cottage cheese .... 1 cup
Ginger-chilli paste .... 1 tbsp
Ghee .... 1 tbsp
Dried mango powder .... 1 tsp
Garam masala .... 1 tsp
Sugar .... 1 tsp
Salt .... 1 tsp

For the Dough
Plain flour, sieved .... 3 cups

Baking powder .... 1 tsp
Sugar .... 1 tsp
Salt .... 1 tsp
Dry yeast .... 1½ tsps
Ghee or butter .... 2 tbsps
Yogurt .... 4 tbsps
Luke warm water .... ½ cup

To Garnish
Chopped green chillies and finely chopped
coriander

METHOD

1. Combine all ingredients for the stuffing in a bowl and mix well. Sieve flour with salt and baking powder. Place it in a large bowl with a well in the centre and set aside.
2. Mix in a small bowl, lukewarm water with dry yeast and sugar and keep it covered in a warm place for ten minutes. When frothy, add it to the flour, along with the *ghee*.
3. Rub the flour with your fingertips to make a dough soft with yogurt and more water if needed. Keep it covered for two hours or until it doubles in volume.
4. Punch down the dough and knead it. Divide into eight parts. Roll out each part in a circle, put two tablespoons of stuffing in each one and close like a ball. Gently press it down and re-roll it like a tear shaped or round shaped.
5. Brush it with a little *ghee* and bake it in a *tandoor* till black specks appear on it. Remove and add coriander and green chillies and put in the *tandoor* again for one minute. Serve hot.

Makes 8 Kulchas

METHI PARATHA
Fenugreek Bread

+++++++++++++++++++++++++++++++++++++++

INGREDIENTS

Fresh fenugreek leaves	1 cup	Turmeric powder	½ tsp
Spring onion, finely chopped	4-5 stems	*Garam masala*	½ tsp
Green chillies, finely chopped	3-4 pieces	Red chilli powder	½ tsp
Wheat flour	1 cup	Salt	to taste
Maize flour	1 cup	*Ghee* to apply and to cook	

METHOD

1. Mix all ingredients (except *ghee*) together and make a soft dough. Set aside for thirty minutes. Divide the dough into walnut sized balls. Roll out a small circle and apply *ghee* on it.
2. Fold it in a triangle and re-roll it to three to four inches. Roast it on the shape of a hot griddle using a little *ghee* around the edges.
3. Turn and roast again. Serve hot with vegetables or yogurt.

Variation: Instead of fenugreek leaves, mint leaves can be used for *pudina* (mint) paratha.

Makes 10-12 parathas

BHATURA
Leavened Fried Bread

+++++++++++++++++++++++++

INGREDIENTS

Plain flour, sieved	1 ½ cups	Soda and salt	a pinch
Yogurt, beaten	½ cup	Oil	for frying

METHOD

1. Combine refined flour, salt and soda. Add yogurt and mix well. Add very little water, knead and prepare pliable dough.
2. Cover with muslin cloth and set aside for six to eight hours.
3. Punch the dough down and make small balls, flatten them on the palm and roll out thick four to five inch round.
4. Heat oil till smoke comes out and fry *bhaturas* on a low flame, one at a time golden brown.
5. Drain and serve hot with Punjabi *chole*.

Makes 4-6

JEERA ALU
Cumin Flavoured Potatoes

+++++++++++++++++++++++++++

INGREDIENTS

Oil..3-4 tbsps
Green chillies, slit 1-2
Cumin seeds .... 1 tsp
A few curry leaves ....
Coriander-cumin powder .... 1 tsp
Chilli powder..................................... 1 tsp
Garam masala .... 1 tsp

Potatoes, washed, peeled and cut into cubes.....
.... 500 gms
Salt .... to taste
Lemon .... to taste

To Garnish
Finely chopped coriander leaves

METHOD

1. Heat oil in a wide pan. Add cumin seeds into it. When they splutter, add green chillies, curry leaves, coriander-cumin powder, chilli powder and garam masala.
2. Fry for two to three minutes. Add the potatoes and mix well. Cover and cook until potatoes are almost done.
3. Add salt and lemon juice to taste. Garnish with coriander leaves and serve with roti or naan.

Serves 4

AACHAR KE AALU
Potatoes in Pickeled Sauce
+++

INGREDIENTS

Potatoes, boiled and cut into 1 inch pieces......... .... 750 gms	Oil .... for frying
Onions, finely chopped .... 5 medium	Salt .... to taste
Ginger-garlic paste .... 2 tbsps	*For Tempering*
Red chilli powder .... 1 tbsp	Oil .... 2 tbsps
Sugar .... 1 tbsp	Cumin seeds .... 1 tsp
Turmeric powder .... ½ tsp	Nigella seeds .... 1 tsp
Vinegar .... ¼ cup	Dry red chillies .... 8 pieces
	Mustard seeds .... ½ tsp

METHOD

1. Fry the potatoes in batches in hot oil and set aside. In a wide pan heat one-third cup of oil and fry onions till golden. Add ginger-garlic paste and fry again. Add chilli powder, turmeric powder and salt. Add the potatoes to the pan.

2. Add half a cup of water and cook on slow flame for five minutes, till spices are well-blended and a little gravy is left.

3. Remove from heat and add vinegar mixed with sugar. Transfer to a serving dish. Heat oil for tempering; add chillies, mustard, cumin and nigella seeds.

4. When mustard seeds begin to splutter, pour it over the potatoes. Serve immediately.

Note: Aachar ke alu *go well with soft buns called* pav.

Serves 6-8

(See photo on page 74)

PANEER MAKHANI
Cottage Cheese Cooked in Butter

+++

INGREDIENTS

For Makhani Gravy

Oil	4 tbsps
Tomatoes, blanched and chopped	500 gms
Red chilli powder	1 tsp
Cardamoms	2-3 pieces
Crushed ginger	2 tbsps
Garlic	2 tbsps
Garam masala	1 tsp
Poppy seeds	1 tbsp
Kasuri methi	1 tsp
Sugar	1 tsp
Fresh cream	¾ cup
Cottage cheese (recipe given below)	500 gms
Butter	50 gms
Crushed ginger and garlic	2 tbsps
Bay leaf	1
Cloves	2-3 pieces
Cinnamon	2-3 pieces
Finely chopped coriander leaves	2-3 tbsps
Salt	to taste

METHOD

FOR THE GRAVY

1. Heat oil in a saucepan; sauté the tomatoes, chilli powder, cloves, cardamom powder, *garam masala*, poppy seeds, ginger-garlic paste and salt. Add one cup of water.
2. Bring this to a boil on a slow flame. Remove when thick. Liquidize this mixture and then put it through a sieve. Add *kasuri methi*, sugar and cream.
3. Set aside. Cut cottage cheese into cubes and sauté them in butter till golden, turning them time-to-time. Remove and drop cottage cheese pieces in water to avoid them from getting chewy.
4. Add this to the tomato gravy, adjust salt and boil for one minute and serve immediately with *naan* or *roti*. Always remember to add cottage cheese pieces just before serving.

Serves 4-6

TO MAKE COTTAGE CHEESE

INGREDIENTS

Full fat milk	1 litre	Yogurt	¼ cup
Lemon juice	2 tsps	Salt	½ tsp

METHOD

1. Heat milk in a saucepan and bring to boil slowly. Gradually add yogurt, lemon juice and salt.
2. Continue stirring gently until milk curdles and separates. Set aside to cool for a few minutes. Strain this through a muslin cloth or fine sieve.
3. Squeeze out remaining liquid.
4. Place with the cloth on a work surface and put weight on it. Set aside for one hour.
5. Cut into pieces and use as required.

Makes 175 gms paneer

DUM ALOO
Spiced Baby Potatoes
+++++++++++++++++++++++++++

INGREDIENTS

Oil...3-4 tbsps
Baby potatoes, washed and soaked in water ....
....500 gms
Salt .... to taste
Sugar .... 1 tsp
Garam masala .... 1 tbsp
Coriander powder..............................1 tbsp
Cumin powder .... 1 tsp
Turmeric powder................................ ½ tsp
Red chilli powder................................ ½ tsp
Tomatoes, liquidized and sieved ...... 4-5 medium
Yogurt... 1 cup

For the Paste

Onions.....................................2 medium

Garlic .... 8-10 cloves
Green chillies .... 4-5 pieces
Ginger .... 1 inch piece
Kashmiri chillies, soaked in water ...... 5-6 pieces
Cinnamon............................... 1 inch piece
Cloves 4-5
Cardamom .... 2-3 pieces
Dry coconut flakes .... ¼ cup
Poppy seeds .... 1 tbsp

To Garnish

Fresh cream and finely chopped coriander leaves

METHOD

1. Roast all ingredients for the paste in oil till a fragrance emanates and make a smooth paste with the help of a little water. Deep-fry the potatoes and prick them with a fork.
2. Set aside. Heat oil in a thick vessel and fry paste until the oil separates. Add salt, *garam masala*, coriander and cumin powder, turmeric powder, red chilli powder and tomato pulp and cook till it starts boiling.
3. Add potatoes, yogurt and sugar. Bring to a boil. Garnish with cream and coriander leaves and serve hot with *naan* or *paratha*.

Serves 4-6

SARSON KA SAAG
Mustard Greens Vegetable

++

INGREDIENTS

Oil .... 6 tbsps	Salt .... to taste
Asafoetida .... a pinch	Maize flour .... 1 tsp
Mustard greens, cleaned and sliced ..... 2 bunches	Onion, grated .... 1 small
Spinach leaves, cleaned and chopped	Ginger, minced .... 1 inch piece
.... ½ bunch	Garlic, minced .... 2 cloves
Turmeric powder .... ½ tsp	Tomato, blanched and chopped .... 1 large
Chilli powder .... to taste	Jaggery .... ½ tbsp

METHOD

1. Heat four tablespoons of oil and asafoetida, add mustard greens, spinach, turmeric powder, chilli powder and salt. Add little water if required.
2. Cover and cook on a slow flame till tender. Remove from fire and cool. Mash the vegetables to a fine paste and return to heat. Mix the maize flour with little water and add to the vegetables.
3. In a small vessel heat two tablespoons of oil and fry onion, ginger and garlic until soft.
4. Add this to the vegetable along with jaggery and mix well. Serve hot with *makai ki roti*.

Serves 4

BHINDI DO PYAZA
Okra with Onions
+++

INGREDIENTS

Oil	4-5 tbsps	Spring onions, sliced (white part only)	2-3 stems
Onions, cut into cubes	2 medium		
Green chillies		Chilli powder	¼ tsp
Okra, washed, pat dried and cut into 1 inch pieces	500 gms	Salt	to taste
Cumin seeds, roasted and ground	1 tsp	**To Garnish**	
Black pepper	¼ tsp	Tomato cut into wedges	1

METHOD

1. Heat three tablespoons of oil in a wide pan, add onions, green chillies and a pinch of salt. Cook till onions are golden brown.
2. Add *okra*, cumin and pepper. Continue frying, stirring from time to time. In another small frying pan heat two tablespoons of oil and fry spring onions with a little salt.
3. Cook until they become soft and add this to the *okra*. Cook until the *okra* is tender. Garnish with tomatoes and serve hot with *rotis*.

Serves 4-6

(See photo on page 74)

BAIGAN BHARTA
Roasted and Mashed Aubergine

+++

INGREDIENTS

Aubergine	2 large	Salt	to taste
Oil	3-4 tbsps	*Garam masala*	1 tbsp
Cumin seeds	1 tsp	Turmeric powder	½ tsp
Oil	3-4 tbsps	Chilli powder	½ tsp
Onions, finely chopped	2 medium	Sugar	½ tsp
Tomatoes, blanched and chopped		***To Garnish***	
	3-4 medium	Finely chopped coriander leaves	

METHOD

1. Prick washed aubergine with a fork and brush it with oil. Roast the aubergine directly on flame or on a barbecue grill until soft. Set aside to cool.
2. Hold it under running water and remove skin. Mash aubergine with a fork. Remove the stem. Set aside.
3. Heat oil in a vessel; sauté cumin seeds, garlic and onion. Cook until soft. Add tomatoes, salt and all the spices. Cook for five to seven minutes.
4. Add the mashed aubergine to it and mix well.
5. Garnish with coriander leaves and serve hot with *naan* or *roti*.

Serves 4-6

(See photo on page 74)

TANDOORI PANEER TIKKA
Cottage Cheese-Vegetable Barbecue
+++

INGREDIENTS

Cottage cheese, cut into cubes .... 500 gms
Green peppers, cut into cubes .... 250 gms
Onions, cut into cubes .... 250 gms
Tomatoes, cut into cubes .... 250 gms
For the Marinade
Thick yogurt .... 1 litre
Ginger-garlic paste (made with 1 inch piece
ginger and 10 cloves garlic) .... 2 tbsps

Tandoori Masala .... 2 tbsps
Garam Masala .... 1 tbsp
Onions, grated 3
Tomatoes, pureed .... 250 gms
Oil .... 5 tbsps
Salt .... to taste
Chilli powder .... to taste

METHOD

1. Heat oil and fry onions till golden brown. Add ginger-garlic paste and fry for one minute. Add tomato puree and spices and fry for two to three minutes.
2. Add yogurt and fry again for three to four minutes. Remove from heat. Add the cottage cheese, peppers and onions. Marinate for three to four hours.
3. Just before cooking, add tomatoes and thread all these alternately on the skewers and then roll them generously into the marinade.
4. Cook on hot grill until vegetables are tender.
5. Serve hot with mint chutney and sliced onions.

<u>Note:</u>   *You can make boiled baby potatoes and cauliflower the same way.*

Serves 6-8

PALAK PANEER
Spinach and Cottage Cheese Vegetable
++++++++++++++++++++++++++++++++

INGREDIENTS

Spinach, cleaned and washed........... 3-4 bunches	Ginger, finely chopped .... 1 inch piece
Ghee ....2-3 tbsps	Green chillies, finely chopped 3
Cottage cheese, cubed .... 250 gms	*Garam masala* .... 1 tsp
Onion, finely chopped .... 1 medium	Salt ....to taste
Tomatoes, grated .... 2 medium	A pinch of soda bi-carbonate
Garlic, chopped .... 2-3 cloves	

METHOD

1. Drop spinach leaves in boiling water with a pinch of soda bi-carbonate. Cook for five to seven minutes. Remove from heat and drain water. Put spinach through the liquidizer and blend until smooth.
2. Heat *ghee* in a wide pan and fry cottage cheese pieces for three to four minutes. Remove and set aside. In the same *ghee* fry onions till pale, add the tomatoes, *garam masala*, garlic, ginger and *chillies*.
3. Cook for further three to four minutes. Add spinach, cottage cheese pieces and salt. Cook uncovered till extra water dries out. Serve hot with *naan*.

Serves 6

MAKAI CURRY
Corn in White Gravy
++++++++++++++++++++++++++++++++

INGREDIENTS

White corn kernels .... 1½ cups	Ginger, finely chopped .... 1 inch piece
Milk ....¾ cup	Scraped coconut...2 tbsps
Oil..1 tbsp	Chopped coriander leaves........................2 tbsps
Cumin seeds .... 1 tsp	Salt .... to taste
Green chillies, finely chopped .... 3-4 pieces	Sugar .... to taste

METHOD

1. Cook corn in a pressure cooker with milk and water and give the cooker three to four whistles. Heat oil in a saucepan and fry cumin seeds.
2. When they splutter, add green chillies and ginger. Cook for two to three minutes. Add the corn, salt and sugar along with the remaining liquid. Cook gently till it gets hot.
3. Add coconut and coriander leaves and serve hot with *roti*.

Serves 4-6

SHAHI PANEER-SABZ MUSALAM
Cottage Cheese and Vegetables Cooked in Red Gravy

+++

INGREDIENTS

Cinnamon powder	½ tsp	Ghee	4 tbsps
Dried red chillies	4	Cashew nuts	2 tbsps
Garlic	5 cloves	Cottage cheese, cut in 2 inch pieces	250 gms
Poppy seeds	2 ½ tsps	Mixed vegetables, cut long and par boiled	
Cloves	8		250 gms
Ginger, finely chopped	1 ½ tbsps	Tomatoes, pureed	4
Cumin seeds	2 ½ tsps	Yogurt and 6 tbsps of cold water together	
Salt	2 ½ tsps		½ cup
Water	6 tbsps	Fresh cream	2 tbsps
Medium sized onions, sliced	2	Coriander leaves, chopped	2 tbsps

METHOD

1. Grind together cinnamon, chillies, garlic, ginger, cloves, cumin, poppy seed, one teaspoon of salt, cashewnuts and water. Process at high speed to make a smooth paste.

2. Sauté onions in *ghee* until they are golden brown. Add them to the blender along with spices and blend until smooth. Reserve the remaining *ghee* in the casserole and set aside.

3. Rub spices onto the cottage cheese and vegetables and marinade for half an hour to one hour. Sprinkle yogurt over it.

4. Reheat *ghee* in the casserole and add cottage cheese and vegetable mixture along with all the liquid accumulated in the plate.

5. Bring to a boil until all the liquid is absorbed. Now add tomatoes and the remaining one and a half teaspoons of salt, transfer into a deep serving dish and garnish with fresh cream and coriander leaves.

Serves 6-8

MALAI METHI MATTAR
Medly of Peas, Fenugreek Leaves and Cream
++

INGREDIENTS

Ghee .... 2 tbsps	Garlic ....2 cloves
Fenugreek leaves, washed and chopped ... 2 cups	Cumin seeds .... 1 tsp
Boiled and shelled peas .... 1 cup	Green chillies ....2 pieces
Home made cream(*Malai*) .... 1 cup	Ginger .... 1 inch piece
Salt .... to taste	**To Garnish**
Sugar .... to taste	Finely chopped coriander leaves
To be ground into paste	
Onion ....1 medium	

METHOD

1. Heat *ghee* in a saucepan; fry the onion, garlic, cumin seeds, green chillies, ginger paste for three to four minutes or until it emits a fragrant aroma. Sprinkle a little water if it sticks to the pan.

2. Add fenugreek leaves and one-fourth cup of water. Cook for three to four minutes. Add the peas, cream, salt and sugar. Gently bring to a boil.

3. Turn it out in a serving dish, garnish with coriander leaves and serve hot with *naan* or *paratha*.

Serves 4

SAMOSAS
Fried Potato Pastries
+++++++++++++++++++++++

INGREDIENTS

For the Pastry

Plain flour .... 1 cup
Ghee .... 1 tbsp
Salt .... ½ tsp
Cold water .... ¼ cup

For the Filling

Oil .... 2 tbsp
Onion, finely chopped .... 1 medium
Finely chopped ginger .... 2 tsps
Cumin seeds .... ½ tsp
Shahjeera .... ½ tsp

Turmeric powder .... ½ tsp
Shelled green peas .... ¼ cup
Potatoes, washed, peeled and cubed ....
.... 2-3 medium
Chopped coriander .... 2 tbsps
Salt .... ½ tsp
Pepper .... ½ tsp
Garam masala .... 1 tsp
Dried mango powder .... 1 tsp
Chilli powder .... 1 tsp
Oil .... for frying

METHOD

FOR THE PASTRY

1. Place the flour, *ghee* and salt in a deep bowl and rub so that it looks like breadcrumbs. Add water to make a soft dough.
2. Knead the dough on a floured surface for two to three minutes, until smooth. Cover with a damp towel and set aside for thirty minutes.

FOR THE FILLING

1. Heat oil in a frying pan and add onion and ginger. Cook for one minute and add cumin seeds, *shahjeera* and turmeric. Then add potatoes, peas, salt and two teaspoons of water.
2. Reduce heat and cook until vegetables are tender. Add *garam masala*, chilli powder, pepper and mango powder. Adjust the seasoning.
3. Add coriander leaves and remove from heat. Transfer to another bowl and set aside to cool at room temperature.
4. To shape the samosas, pinch off a small dough into a semi circle cone and roll it to a three to four inch round disc. Cut it from the centre.
5. Moisten the edges with water and shape the dough sealing both the corners tightly.
6. Fill this with one tablespoon of potato filling and press the top edges together to seal.
7. Cover with foil and repeat the same procedure for the remaining dough and the filling.
8. Fry samosas in hot oil four to five pieces at a time until golden brown on all sides. Serve hot with *chutney*.

Makes 20-24 samosas

GAJAR KA AACHAR
North Indian Style Carrot Pickle
++

INGREDIENTS

Carrots, peeled and cut into sticks .... 2 cups	Split mustard grains .... 2 tbsps
Beetroot, blanched and cut into sticks	Salt .... 2 tbsps
.... 1 medium	Vinegar .... 4 tbsps
Raw mango, peeled and cubed .... 1 medium	Green chillies, slit .... 4-5 pieces
Lemon, cut into 8 pieces .... 1 large	Mustard oil .... 1 cup
Shallots, peeled .... 8-10 pieces	Turmeric powder .... a pinch

METHOD

1. Soak onions in vinegar overnight. Mix all ingredients except oil, in a bowl and toss gently.
2. Fill this in a jar and pour hot and also cool oil to coat the vegetables. Use after three to four days.

`Makes ½ kg`

KAIRI KA ABHOSLA
Raw Mango Sherbet
++

INGREDIENTS

Raw mangoes .... 1 kg	Fresh mint leaves 15-20
Powdered sugar .... ½-¾ cup	A pinch of salt
Roasted cumin powder .... 2 tbsps	

METHOD

1. Pressure-cook whole raw mangoes. Discard water. Peel mangoes and squeeze the pulp out.
2. Discard seeds. Chill the pulp. Blend together chilled pulp, sugar, cumin powder and mint leaves in a liquidizer jar.
3. Add a little water if needed. Pour it out in glasses filled with ice.

`Serves 10`

GAJAR HALVA
Carrot Sweet
+++++++++++++++++++++++++++++++++

INGREDIENTS

Carrots, scraped and coarsely grated......500 gms	Cardamom seeds, powdered .... ½ tsp
Milk .... 3 cups	**To Garnish**
Sugar .... 1 cup	Slivered and toasted almonds
Ghee .... 3 tbsps	Pistachios
Blanched and chopped almonds ....½ cup	Varakh
Cream ....½ cup	

METHOD

1. Put carrots, milk and cream in a thick saucepan. Bring to a boil over high heat, stirring constantly. Continue cooking till the mixture is reduced to half its volume.

2. Stir in sugar and continue cooking for ten more minutes. Reduce heat to the lowest possible point, add *ghee* and almonds.

3. Cook further till the *halva* is thick enough to draw away from the sides of the pan. Remove from heat and add cardamom.

4. Spread *halva* on a large serving dish and decorate with nuts and *varakh*. Serve warm or at room temperature.

Serves 6-8

MULLIGATAWNY SOUP

Curry Flavoured Lentil Soup

+++

INGREDIENTS

Butter	1 tbsp	Water	4 cups
Onion, chopped	2 medium	Curry powder	1 tsp
Bottle gourd	250 gms	Salt	to taste
Garlic	2 cloves	Pepper	to taste
Carrots, chopped	2 medium	**To Serve**	
Tomatoes	2	Pieces of lemon	
Red lentils, washed and soaked	4 tbsps	Steamed rice	

METHOD

1. Melt butter in a pan and sauté onions and garlic. Add all vegetables, lentils and four cups of water and cook it in the pressure cooker and give it four whistles.
2. Let it cool and put it in the liquidizer and then strain. Return to heat. Add curry powder, salt and pepper and boil until thick. Serve hot with lemon pieces and rice.

Serves 4

TOMATO RASAM

Spicy Tomato Water

+++++++++++++++++++++++++++++++++

INGREDIENTS

Ghee	1 tbsp	Salt	to taste
Black peppercorns	8-10	Tamarind pulp	2 tsps
Cumin seeds	1½ tsp	Jaggery or ½ tsp of sugar	1 tsp
Tomatoes, blanched	2 large	Mustard seeds	½ tsp
Dry red chillies, roasted	1	Asafoetida	2 pinches
Coriander leaves, finely chopped	1 tbsp	Garlic, chopped	2 cloves
Cinnamon powder	2-3 pinches	Red split gram water	4 cups
Clove powder	2-3 pinches	Curry leaves	a few
Rasam powder	1 tbsp		

METHOD

1. Heat half a teaspoon of *ghee* and roast peppercorns and one teaspoon of cumin seeds, grind in a mortar till powdered and keep aside.
2. Grate tomatoes. Add red chillies, coriander leaves, cinnamon and clove powder, *rasam* powder, salt, tamarind and jaggery. Blend all this with tomatoes to a thick pulp.
3. In a saucepan heat *ghee*, add mustard, half a teaspoon of cumin seeds, curry leaves, asafoetida and allow it to splutter. Add garlic and stir in carefully with the tomato mixture.
4. Add split gram water and put in spices and salt. Simmer for three to four minutes and serve hot.

Note: *To make four cups split gram water, cook half cup split gram with four cups of water in pressure cooker. Churn and used as required.*

Serves 6

MASALA DOSA VADA
Potato Filled Pancake Dumplings
+++

INGREDIENTS

Dosa batter (recipe on page ...) .... 2 cups
Potato vegetable for *dosa* (recipe given below) ..
.... 2 cups
Oil .... for frying

Salt .... to taste

To Serve
Coconut *chutney* (recipe on page 103)

METHOD

1. Make small balls of the *dosa* vegetable. Heat oil.
2. Dip each ball in the *dosa* batter and fry it on medium heat in hot oil until golden brown. Serve hot with coconut *chutney*.

Makes 15-20 dumplings

POTATO VEGETABLE FOR DOSA

INGREDIENTS

Potatoes (medium sized) boiled & peeled 8
Cumin seeds .... 1 tsp
Mustard seeds .... 1 tsp
Split white gram .... 1 tsp
Bengal gram .... 1 tsp
Green chillies, chopped 5-6
Ginger .... 1 inch piece

Curry leaves .... a few
Turmeric powder .... ½ tsp
Onions, cut into thin slices 4
Coriander leaves .... ½ cup
Juice of lemon 1
Oil .... 3-4 tbsps
Salt .... to taste

METHOD

1. Cut potatoes into small cubes.
2. Heat oil in a wide pan, add cumin and mustard seeds, white gram and bengal gram. Fry for a minute. Add green chillies, ginger, curry leaves and turmeric powder.
3. Add onions and cook until they are transperant. Add potatoes and salt. Mix well.
4. Sprinkle corinder leaves and lemon juice.
5. Serve hot with *dosa*.

Makes 4-5 cups

STEAMED IDLIES
Steamed Rice and Lentil Cakes
++++++++++++++++++++++++++++++++++++

INGREDIENTS

Raw rice	3 cups	Oil to grease the mould
Parboiled rice	1 cup	**To Serve**
White split lentils	1¼ cups	Sambhar, *molgaipudi* and coconut *chutney*
Salt	to taste	(recipes on pages 104, 103)

METHOD

1. Soak both the rice in boiling water for six hours. Soak lentils separately for six hours. Grind rice coarsely and lentils finely.
2. Mix both together, add salt and set aside for fermentation overnight. Next morning smear the *idli* moulds with little oil and pour one-fourth cup of batter in each mould.
3. Steam idlies in a steamer for seven to ten minutes. Serve hot with *sambhar*, *chutney* or *molgaipudi*.

Makes 16 idlies

DOSA
Rice and Lentil Pancakes
+++++++++++++++++++++++++

INGREDIENTS

Par boiled rice	3 cups	Oil or butter to cook
White split lentils	¾ cup	**To Serve**
Fenugreek seeds	2 tsps	Sambhar, coconut *chutney* and potato
Salt	to taste	vegetable (recipes on pages104, 103 & 97)

METHOD

1. Soak rice in boiling water for six hours. Soak lentils separately for six hours with fenugreek seeds.
2. Grind rice and lentils separately to a fine paste. Mix both together, add salt and set aside for fermentation overnight.
3. Next morning mix the batter thoroughly. Heat a flat griddle and smear it with little oil. Pour a large spoonful of batter and spread as thinly as possible into a circle. Rub little butter over the top and around the edges.
4. When cooked, scrape it from the edges and turn over. Cook the other side. Serve with *sambhar*, coconut *chutney* and potato vegetable.

Makes 12 dosas

BISI BELE HULIYANNA
Rice and Lentils in Spicy Sauce
+++

INGREDIENTS

Yellow lentils, washed and soaked .... 1 cup
Rice, washed and soaked in water .... 500 gms
Tamarind juice .... ½ cup
Salt .... to taste
Mustard seeds .... 1 tsp
Curry leaves .... a few
Cashewnuts.. 2 tbsps
Tomatoes, chopped .... 2-3 medium
Oil.. 4 tbsps

For the Spices to be Ground
Coriander seeds.. 2 tbsps
Dry red chillies .... 12 pieces

Grated coconut .... 1 cup
White split grams .... 1 tsp
Yellow split grams .... 1 tsp
Turmeric .... 1 tsp
Fenugreek seeds .... ½ tsp
Garam masala .... ½ tsp
A pinch of asafoetida

To Garnish
Finely chopped coriander leaves and spicy potato wafers

To Serve
Melted *ghee*

METHOD

1. Cook lentils in three cups of water until soft. Dry roast spices and grind them to a fine powder. Add washed rice to cooked lentils and cook again till soft.
2. Add tamarind juice, powdered spices and salt. Mix well. Cook with just enough water so that the mixture is semi-dry when cooked.
3. Heat oil in a small pan, add mustard seeds, curry leaves, cashews and tomatoes. Cook until tomatoes are soft. Pour this over rice and lentil mixture.
4. Mix well. Serve piping hot with coriander leaves, wafers and melted *ghee*.

Serves 6-8

MEDU WADA

Lentil Balls

++++++++++++++++++++++++++++++++

INGREDIENTS

White split gram .... 1¾ cups

Yellow split gram .... ¼ cup

Green chillies, chopped .... 4 pieces

A pinch of asafoetida and soda-bi-carbonate

Salt .... to taste

Oil .... for frying

To Serve

Coconut *chutney* and *sambhar*

(recipes on pages 103 & 104)

METHOD

1. Soak both grams in water for eight hours. Drain and grind to a smooth paste. Add chillies, asafoetida, soda and salt. Add two tablespoons of hot water.

2. Mix thoroughly in an upward movement to make batter light and fluffy. Make lemon-sized balls and flatten them on your palm.

3. Make a hole in the centre of each one and fry them in hot oil, four to five at a time. Fry till golden brown.

4. Drain on a kitchen paper and serve hot with coconut *chutney* and *sambhar*.

Note: *You may add one finely chopped onion and one tablespoon of chopped coriander leaves to gram mixture before frying.*

Serves 6-8

COCONUT CHUTNEY

+++

INGREDIENTS

Scraped fresh coconut	2 cups	Salt	to taste
Green chillies	2 pieces	*For Tempering*	
Bengal gram, soaked	1 tbsp	Oil	2 tbsps
Sugar or jaggery	1 tbsp	Mustard seeds	½ tsp
Tamarind pulp	1 tbsp	White split gram	½ tsp
Ginger	1 inch piece	Asafoetida	¼ tsp
Garlic (optional)	1 clove	A few curry leaves	

METHOD

1. Grind all ingredients together in a small grinder with little water to a fine paste.
2. Heat oil in a small vessel and add mustard seeds. When they splutter, add white split gram, asafoetida and curry leaves.
3. Pour this over the prepared *chutney* and serve with south Indian snacks.

Makes 1½ cups

MOLGAIPUDI
Dry Powdered Chutney

++++++++++++++++++++++++++++++

INGREDIENTS

White split gram	½ cup	Asafoetida	½ tsp
Bengal split gram	½ cup	Curry leaves	a few
Dry red chillies	8-10 pieces	Oil	¼ cup
Grated dry coconut	½ cup	Salt	to taste

METHOD

1. Fry both varieties of gram, chillies and coconut separately in little oil till golden brown. Add salt and asafoetida to roasted ingredients.
2. Grind them coarsely and fill in a jar. Use as required.

<u>*Note:*</u>   *This keeps well for two to three weeks.*

Makes ¾ cups

SAMBHAR
Spiced Lentil with Vegetables
++++++++++++++++++++++++++++

INGREDIENTS

Split yellow or orange lentils, washed and soaked
.... 1 cup
Turmeric powder .... ½ tsp
Oil .... 2-3 tbsps
Mustard seeds .... ½ tsp
White split grams .... ½ tsp
Onion, chopped .... 3-4 pieces
A few curry leaves ....
Sambhar powder (recipe given below) ..... 2 tbsps
Red onions, peeled .... 6-8 small

Water .... 3 cups
Tomatoes, chopped .... 3-4 pieces
Bottle gourd, cut into cubes and boiled ....
.... 1 small piece
Drum sticks, cut into 2 inch pieces and boiled .
.... 1-2 pieces
Potato, peeled and cubed and boiled ....
.... 1 medium
Tamarind water .... ¼ cup
Salt .... to taste

METHOD

1. Cook lentil with turmeric, onions and water in a pressure cooker and give it three to four whistles or for fifteen to twenty minutes.
2. Heat oil in a saucepan; add mustard seeds and white split grams. When they splutter, add onions, curry leaves and *sambhar* powder. Cook till it emits a fragrance. Add tomatoes and salt along with boiled vegetables.
3. Add cooked lentils from the pressure cooker along with water. Bring to boil and simmer till it is slightly thickened. Add tamarind water and simmer for five to ten minutes more.
4. Serve hot with *idli*, *dosa* or any south Indian dish as an accompaniment.

Serves 6

SAMBHAR POWDER

INGREDIENTS

Coriander seeds .... 3 tbsps
Split Bengal gram .... 1 tbsp
Fenugreek seeds .... ½ tsp
Dried red chillies .... 6-8 pieces

Asafoetida .... 1 tsp
Turmeric powder .... 1 tsp
Grated dry coconut .... ¼ cup
Oil .... 1 tbsp

METHOD

1. Roast all the ingredients in oil on a thick griddle till a fragrance emanates. Remove from heat and set aside to cool.
2. Grind them to a fine powder and fill in an airtight jar and use as required.

Makes ¾ cup

VEGETABLE UPMA

Semolina Savoury

╋╋╋╋╋╋╋╋╋╋╋╋╋╋╋╋╋╋╋╋╋╋╋╋╋╋╋╋╋╋╋╋╋╋╋╋╋╋╋

INGREDIENTS

Semolina (*Rawa*) .... 1 cup

Water .... 1¾ cups

Mixed vegetables .... ½

Salt .... to taste

Juice of ½ a lemon ....

For Tempering

Ghee ....3-4 tbsps

Onion, finely chopped .... 1 medium

Tomato, finely chopped .... 1 medium

Mustard seeds .... 1 tsp

Yellow split gram .... 1 tsp

White split gram .... 1 tsp

Cashew nuts, broken into pieces .... 4-5 pieces

Green chillies, roughly chopped .... 3-4 pieces

Curry leaves .... a few

To Garnish

Finely chopped coriander leaves and grated coconut.

METHOD

1. Roast semolina on a medium flame till light golden. Set aside to cool. In a wide pan, heat *ghee*; add mustard seeds, yellow and white split gram, cashew nuts, curry leaves and green chillies.

2. Fry for two minutes, stirring all the time. Add onions and cook until soft. Add tomato, vegetables and salt. Mix well. Very slowly, add semolina in a thin stream.

3. Cook again for two minutes, stirring all the time. Remove from fire and add water, stirring continuously. Return to heat and cook gently till the mixture is thick.

4. Add lemon juice and adjust salt. Garnish with coriander and grated coconut. Serve hot as a breakfast dish.

Serves 4

THAIR SADAM
Yogurt Rice
++++++++++++++++++++++++++++++++

INGREDIENTS

Raw rice, washed and soaked in water ...... 2 cups	Yogurt .... 3½ cups
Oil or *ghee* .... 2 tbsps	Milk .... 3-4 tbsps
Mustard seeds .... ½ tsp	Salt .... to taste
Green chillies, chopped .... 3-4 pieces	**To Serve**
Ginger, chopped .... ½ inch piece	Spicy Lemon pickle (recipe given below)
Curry leaves .... a few	

METHOD

1. Cook rice in four cups of water with little salt until soft and set aside. Heat oil or *ghee* and fry mustard seeds, green chillies, ginger and curry leaves.
2. Mash rice slightly and add fried spices over it. Beat yogurt with little salt and mix with rice.
3. Add milk and mix thoroughly. Serve with lemon pickle.

SPICY LEMON PICKLE
++

INGREDIENTS

Whole lemons .... 25 large	Salt .... ½ kg
Green chillies .... 100 gms	Juice of 5 lemons
Ginger .... 100 gms	**For Tempering**
Red chilli powder .... 100 gms	Oil .... 1 tsp
Turmeric powder .... 2 tbsps	Mustard seeds .... 1 tsp
Split mustard grains .... 2 tbsps	Asafoetida .... 1 tsp
Sugar .... 100 gms	

METHOD

1. Wash and drop lemons in boiling water. Cut each lemon into eight parts. Wash and chop green chillies and ginger into half inch pieces.
2. Mix together chilli powder, turmeric powder, split mustard grains, sugar and salt in a bowl. Take a clean glass jar and layer lemon pieces, chillies, ginger and dry spices.
3. Heat oil for tempering, add mustard seeds and when they splutter, add asafoetida. Take it off heat and add this to lemon mixture. Mix well.
4. Cover and set aside for three to four days to marinate. Use as required.

Makes 1½ kg

SABZI PANCHMELA

Medley of Five Vegetables

++

INGREDIENTS

Potatoes	200 gms	Garam masala	2 tbsps
Red pumpkin	200 gms	Cashew nuts	1 tbsp
Brinjal	200 gms	Poppy seeds	1 tbsp
Onion	200 gms	Coriander powder	1 tbsp
Green leafy vegetable	200 gms	Cumin powder	1 tbsp
Ghee	3-4 tbsps	Garlic	5 cloves
Salt	to taste	Dry red chillies, soaked in water	7-8 pieces
Sugar	to taste	Ginger, grated	½ inch piece
Water	1 cups		

For the Paste

Powdered mustard seeds .... 2 tbsps

To Garnish

3-4 tbsps of thick cream and finely chopped coriander leaves

METHOD

1. Grind all the ingredients for the paste together with little water and set aside.
2. Cut potatoes, pumpkin, brinjal and onions in cubes and soak them in water. Tear green leaves into square pieces.
3. Heat *ghee* in a heavy saucepan or a wide pan. Fry the paste until fragrant. Add all vegetables (except greens), salt, sugar and water. Cover and cook until vegetables are soft.
4. Now add greens and bring to a boil. Mix gram flour in a little water and add to vegetables. Boil till gravy is thick.
5. Garnish with cream and chopped coriander leaves. Serve with *roti*.

Serves 6-8

DAL
Spiced Lentils
+++++++++++++++++++

INGREDIENTS

Split red gram	¼ cup	Cumin seeds	½ tsp
Split Bengal gram	¼ cup	Cloves	5 pieces
Black gram	¼ cup	Cardamoms	5 pieces
Green gram	¼ cup	Bay leaves	3-4 pieces
Yellow split gram	½ cup	Ginger, sliced	1 inch piece
Salt	1 tsp	Fenugreek	½ tsp
Chilli powder	2 tsps	Round Red chillies	3-4 pieces
Sugar	1 tsp	Asafoetida	¼ tsp
Ghee	4 tbsps	Turmeric	½ tsp
Garam masala	2 tsps	**To Garnish**	
Mustard seeds	1 tsp	Finely chopped coriander leaves	

METHOD

1. Wash grams and soak for fifteen to twenty minutes. Boil three to four cups of water and add all the soaked gram along with turmeric powder, salt, chilli powder, sugar and one tablespoon of *ghee*.
2. Cook until grams are soft. Stir in *garam masala* powder. Simmer *dal* till it becomes thick.
3. In another small pan, heat three tablespoons of *ghee* and add mustard seeds, cumin seeds, cloves, cardamoms, bay leaves, ginger, fenugreek, red chillies and asafoetida.
4. Cook for one minute and add this to the cooked *dal*. Mix well.
5. Serve hot with *bati*.

Serves 4-6

BATI
Roasted Whole Wheat Cakes
++++++++++++++++++++++++++

INGREDIENTS

Whole wheat flour, sieved .... 750 gms	Soda-bi-carbonate .... 1 tsp
Ghee .... 5 tbsps	Hot water .... 250 ml
Salt .... 2 tsps	Hot *ghee* .... 1 cup
Sugar .... 1 tsp	

METHOD

1. Mix flour with five tablespoons of *ghee*, salt, sugar and soda-bi-carbonate. Make a stiff dough with one cup of hot water. Knead the dough well and set aside for one hour.
2. Make walnut sized balls and flatten each one like a patty. Pinch each one from the sides like pleats. Boil plenty of water in a steamer and arrange the *bati* in a single layer on a plate.
3. Cover and steam for twenty minutes. Remove from fire and spread them out on a dry surface to cool. Roast them over an open flame like a grill or bake them in a hot oven till brown.
4. Soak them in hot *ghee* for about five to seven minutes and serve with *dal*.

Makes 20 batis

MIRCHI VADA
Chilli Fritters
++++++++++++++++++++++++++++++++

INGREDIENTS

Big size green chillies	12 pieces	Chopped coriander leaves	2 tbsps

For the Stuffing

For the Batter

Mashed potatoes	1 cup	Gram flour	1 cup
Salt	1 tsp	Water	1 cup
Chaat masala	1 tsp	Baking powder	½ tsp
Chilli powder	1 tsp	Salt	½ tsp
Garam masala	1 tsp	Chilli powder	½ tsp
Dried mango powder	1 tsp	Oil	for frying

METHOD

1. Wash and slit chillies from the centre, remove seeds and set aside. Mix together all the ingredients for the stuffing.

2. Stuff chillies with this mixture. Use one to two tablespoons of mixture for each one depending on the size. Mix all the ingredients for the batter, to make a smooth mixture.

3. Dip each chilli in this batter to give a thick coat. Deep fry *vada* in hot oil till golden in colour. Serve at once.

Serves 6

(See photo on page 113)

MASALA PAPAD
Spicy Papadam
++++++++++++++++++++++++++++++++++

INGREDIENTS

Bikaneri Papads	6 large	Green chillies, finely chopped	2-3 small
Oil	for frying	Finely chopped coriander leaves	¼ cup
For sprinkling on top		Chilli powder	1 tsp
Onions, finely chopped	2 medium	Dried mango powder	1 tsp
Tomatoes, finely chopped	2 medium		

METHOD

1. Heat oil in frying pan and fry the *papadams*, one at a time and drain on paper towel. Wipe coriander and chillies with a towel to dry them completely.
2. Arrange one *papadam* at a time on a plate and sprinkle with onions, tomatoes, chillies, coriander and spices. Serve at once.

Serves 6

(See photo on page 113)

DATE AND TAMARIND CHUTNEY
+++

INGREDIENTS

Deseeded and chopped dates	1 cup	Coriander powder	1 tsp
Tamarind, cleaned	½ cup	Salt	1 tsp
Chilli powder	1 tsp	Black salt	½ tsp
Cumin powder	1 tsp	A pinch of asafoetida	

METHOD

1. Mix all ingredients together in a saucepan with half a cup of water. Cook until dates are soft, stirring from time to time.
2. Set aside to cool. Put all ingredients in the liquidizer and blend to a smooth paste.
3. Pass it through a sieve and add little water and salt if required.

Makes 1½ cups

DAHI VADA
Lentil Balls Marinated in Yogurt
+++++++++++++++++++++++++++++++

INGREDIENTS

For the Vada
Black or white split gram, washed and soaked ....
overnight .... 1 cup
Ginger-chilli paste ....1 tbsp
Baking powder ....1 tsp
Salt .... to taste
Oil for frying
For the Dahi
Thick yogurt.. 500 ml
Salt .... 1 tsp

Sugar .... 1 tsp
Cumin powder .... 1 tsp
Chilli powder .... 1 tsp
Finely chopped coriander leaves .... 1 tbsp
To Garnish
A few pomegranate seeds
Crisp potato sticks
To Serve
Date and tamarind chutney (recipe on page 111)

METHOD

1. Grind grams to a fine paste with minimum water. Mix ginger-chilli paste, baking powder and salt. Mix well by beating vigorously.
2. Heat oil on high for frying and then put on medium heat. Make your palms a little wet with water and take a little mixture to form a walnut sized ball.
3. Flatten it slightly and deep-fry them in hot oil until golden brown. Drain on kitchen paper. Drop these balls in warm water and let it stand for fifteen minutes.
4. Squeeze out water and place them on a serving dish.

FOR THE DAHI

1. Beat yogurt with a beater until smooth. Add remaining ingredients and pour it over the *vadas* arranged on a plate.
2. Garnish them with pomegranate seeds and potato sticks. Chill until ready to serve. Serve with *chutney*.

Serves 6-8

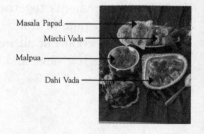

Masala Papad
Mirchi Vada
Malpua
Dahi Vada

SAAT PADI ROTI - GATTE KA SAAK

Layered Bread With Flour Dumpling Vegetable

++

INGREDIENTS

For the Roti

Whole wheat flour, sieved	1 cup
Plain flour, sieved	½ cup
Spicy mango pickle	1 tbsp
Chopped coriander leaves	1 tbsp
Turmeric powder	½ tsp
Salt	½ tsp
Melted *ghee*	2 tbsps
Ghee for applying and frying	3-4 tbsps

For the Gatta

Gram flour, sieved	1 cup
Chilli powder	1 tsp
Asafoetida	½ tsp
Salt	½ tsp
Oil	2 tsps
Yogurt	2 tsps

Boiling water	2 cups

For the Gravy

Sour yogurt	1 cup
Water	1 cup
Gram flour	1 tsp
Ghee	1 tbsp
Coriander leaves	1 tbsp
Bay leaf	1
Chilli powder	1 tsp
Salt	1 tsp
Turmeric powder	½ tsp
Coriander-cumin powder	½ tsp
Cumin seeds	½ tsp
Dried mango powder	½ tsp
Garam masala	½ tsp
A few curry leaves and round red chillies	

METHOD

FOR THE ROTI

1. Mix both the flours, make a well in the centre and pour hot *ghee* in it. Cover with flour and set aside for five to ten minutes. Mix *ghee* and flour.
2. Add salt, pickle, turmeric powder and coriander. Make a semi-soft dough and set aside for half an hour. Roll out a big circle from this dough to one-fourth inch thickness. Apply *ghee* with your fingertips all around to cover the dough.
3. Roll this in the shape of a flute in jelly roll fashion. Cut in half inch discs. Take one, press slightly with your palm and roll each one to five inch round.
4. Roast it on a hot griddle with the help of little *ghee*, turning it on both sides. Serve hot with *gatte ka saak*.

FOR THE GATTA

1. Mix gram flour, chilli powder, asafoetida and salt. Add oil, yogurt and enough water to make a stiff dough. Take one-fourth cup of dough at a time and roll it into thin cylindrical shaped sticks.
2. Drop them in boiling water. When they come up to the surface, remove from water and let it dry a little on a cutting board.

1. Heat *ghee* in a saucepan; add cumin seeds, chillies, curry leaves and bay leaf. Add yogurt and water mixture. Now add all the spices and *gatta* pieces. Bring to a boil and simmer till the gravy is thick.
2. Adjust seasoning. Serve hot with *roti*.
   (If you like slight sweetness in your food, you can add half a teaspoon of sugar)

Serves 4-6

DAHI KE ALU
Potatoes with Yogurt
+++++++++++++++++++++++++++++++

INGREDIENTS

Potatoes, peeled and cut into cubes .... 500 gms	*For Dry Spices*
Thick yogurt .... 2 cups	Coriander-cumin powder .... 1 tbsp
Chick pea flour .... 1 tbsp	Red chilli powder .... 1 tsp
For Tempering	Turmeric powder .... ½ tsp
Oil .... ¼ cup	*Garam masala* .... ½ tsp
Mustard seeds .... 1 tsp	Salt .... to taste
Asafoetida .... ¼ tsp	*To Garnish*
Curry leaves .... a few	Finely chopped coriander leaves and hot *ghee*
Kashmiri red chillies .... 3-4 pieces	mixed with chilli powder

METHOD

1. Heat oil in pan, add mustard seeds, asafoetida, dry red chillies and curry leaves. Fry for one minute.
2. Add potatoes along with all the dry spices. Cover and cook on a slow flame till potatoes are soft.
3. Pour a little water on the cover to prevent the potatoes from sticking to the pan. Mix chick-pea flour with yogurt and add this mixture to the potatoes.
4. Bring to a boil and summer till the gravy gets thick.
5. Garnish with coriander leaves and *ghee* with chilli powder.

Serves 4-6

KANJIVADA
++++++++++++++++++++++++

INGREDIENTS

Make the *vada* as per the recipe for *Dahi vada* (recipe on page 112) and soak them in mustard water (recipe given below) instead of yogurt.

For Mustard Water (*Kanji*)

Cold water	3 cups	Salt	½ tsp
Split mustard seeds, ground	2 tbsps	Asafoetida	½ tsp
Ginger-chilli paste	1 tbsp	Juice of 1 lemon	
Finely chopped coriander	1 tbsp	**To Garnish**	
Chilli powder	½ tsp	Finely chopped coriander leaves	
Black salt	½ tsp		

METHOD

1. Make lentil balls as per *dahi vada* recipe and soak them in water.
2. Mix all the ingredients for mustard water in a deep bowl and drop soaked and drained lentil balls into it.
3. Cover and keep for six to eight hours to marinate. Garnish with coriander leaves and serve in individual bowls as an appetizer.

Serves 6-8

MALPUA
Fried Pancake in Syrup
+++++++++++++++++++++++++

INGREDIENTS

Milk, boiled and reduced to half .... 1 litre
Saffron .... a few threads
Sieved Together
Plain flour .... 2-3 tbsps
Baking powder .... ¼ tsp
Powdered sugar .... 2 tbsps

Cardamom powder .... a pinch
Ghee for frying
Thinly sliced pistachios .... 2-3 tbsps
Thinly sliced almonds .... 2-3 tbsps
Whole sugar .... 250 gms

METHOD

1. Mix milk and plain flour mixed with baking powder and two tablespoons of sugar. Cover and set aside. Mix remaining sugar with water and boil to make a thick syrup.
2. Add saffron and cardamom powder and keep warm in a serving dish. While frying the pancake, if you feel the batter is too thin, add a little more flour to gain thick, pouring consistency.
3. In a small frying pan, add one teaspoon of *ghee* and pour one teaspoon of the flour-milk mixture and cook till golden. Turn over and cook the other side as well.
4. Fold over to make a half-moon shape. Place on a serving plate over the syrup.
5. Repeat till all the pancakes are done. Sprinkle with chopped pistachios and almonds and serve hot.

<u>*Note:*</u>   *To make orange malpua, mix a little orange juice along with water to make the syrup and add grated orange rind instead of saffron and cardamom. Add half a teaspoon of orange essence to the batter.*

Serves 6

(See photo on page 113)

PANEER KATHI KABABS
Spicy Cottage Cheese Wrap
+++

INGREDIENTS

Cottage cheese, cubed	250 gms	Onion, grated	1 medium
Onion	1 piece	Tomato purée	¼ cup
Tomato	1 piece	Salt	to taste
Oil	2 + 1 tbsp	Yogurt, beaten	1 cup
Tandoori masala	2-3 tbsps	**To Serve**	
Ginger paste	2-3 tbsps	Sliced onions, freshly chopped coriander,	
Garlic paste	2-3 tbsps	lemon wedges and coriander-mint *chutney*	
Red chilli paste	1 tbsp	*Roomali rotis* (recipe given below)	3 large

METHOD

1. Mix together cottage cheese with onion and tomato in a wide bowl. In a frying pan, heat two tablespoon of oil and add *tandoori masala*, ginger-garlic, chilli paste and grated onion.
2. Fry for three to four minutes. Add tomato purée, salt and yogurt. Mix well. Remove from heat and pour over the cottage cheese and vegetables.
3. Cover and keep aside for forty-five minutes or more. Grease a frying pan or a baking dish with one tablespoon of oil. Either sauté the cottage cheese and vegetables or grill them until golden brown.
4. To serve, take one warmed *roomali roti*, place it on the flat surface and spoon one-third of the mixture at one end of the *roti*. Roll or wrap and fold the ends.
5. Serve immediately with sliced onions, coriander, lemon wedges and green *chutney*.

`Serves 6`

ROOMALI ROTI

1. Make the dough with one cup of strong plain flour, half a teaspoon of salt, one tablespoon of oil and one-third cup of warm water. Cover and set aside for forty-five minutes.
2. Knead it again and divide into three parts. Roll out each one paper-thin. Invert a heavy cast iron pan over the burner and spread the *roti* over it.
3. Cook for forty-five to fifty seconds. Remove, fold it into one-fourth and set aside in a thin napkin or use immediately.

PANEER LIFAFA
Cottage Cheese Envelope
++++++++++++++++++++++++++++++++

INGREDIENTS

Wheat flour	150 gms	Finely chopped mint leaves	½ cup
Plain flour	150 gms	Coriander and mint *chutney* (recipe on page.....)	
Ghee	2 tbsps		½ cup
Milk to bind the dough		Cottage cheese, cut into 1 inch	300 gms
A pinch of salt		*Ghee*	4 tbsps
For the Filling		*To Serve*	
Jeeralu powder	2 tsps	Yogurt and cucumber *raita*	
Onions, finely chopped	2 small		

METHOD

1. Mix both flours together with a little salt and add two tablespoons of *ghee*. Bind soft dough with milk. Cover and set aside for half an hour.
2. Sprinkle one teaspoon of *jeeralu* over the cottage cheese pieces and set aside. Mix together onions, mint leaves, one teaspoon of jeeralu and one tablespoon of green chutney. Set aside.
3. Make twelve to fifteen balls of the dough and roll each one to seven inch round. Slightly roast the rotis on both sides on a hot griddle. Spread one tablespoon of chutney on the border of each round.
4. Sprinkle onion mixture evenly in the centre. Arrange three pieces of cottage cheese in a criss-cross manner on the top. Now fold the circle in four ways like an envelope.
5. Fry on a non-stick frying pan with the help of a little *ghee* poured around each envelope. Cook both sides and serve hot with yogurt-cucumber *raita*.

Serves 6

YOGURT CUCUMBER RAITA

INGREDIENTS

Thick yogurt	1 cup	Salt	to taste
Green chilli, chopped	2 small	Sugar	to taste
Cucumber sliced	1 medium		

METHOD

1. Mix all the ingredients together and chill until ready to serve.

CHILLI-PANEER
Cottage Cheese with Chillies

+++++++++++++++++++++++++++++++++

INGREDIENTS

Plain flour	1 tsp	Garlic, crushed	4-5 cloves
Corn flour	1 tsp	Salt	½ tsp
Salt	½ tsp	Pepper	½ tsp
Cottage cheese, cut into one inch pieces 200 gms		Sugar	½ tsp
		Chilli sauce	1 tbsp
Butter	2 tsps	Vinegar	½ tbsp
Oil	2 tsps	Spring onions, cut long	2 stems
Green chillies, slit length wise	4-5	Finely chopped coriander leaves	1 tbsp
Crushed ginger	1 tbsp		

METHOD

1. Mix plain flour, corn flour and salt. Roll cottage cheese pieces in this mixture. Set aside. In a frying pan heat butter and oil together and fry green chillies, ginger, and garlic.
2. Add salt, pepper, sugar and chilli sauce, vinegar and stir. Add a little water to avoid sticking.
3. Add cottage cheese, spring onions and coriander and mix well. Serve hot with a toothpick stuck on to each piece.

Note: *You may use pieces of vegetables like baby corn and mushrooms alongwith cottage cheese.*

Serves 4

(See photo on page 124)

DHAN-SAAK BROWN RICE
Split Grams and Vegetables Cooked in Parsi Style with Sweetened Rice

+++

INGREDIENTS

For Dhan-saak

Split red gram (*Tuvar dal*)	1 cup
Yellow split gram	1 tbsp
White split gram	1 tbsp
Orange split gram	1 tbsp
Split field beans	1 tbsp
Potato	1 medium
Brinjal	1 small
Red pumpkin (2 inch to 3 inch)	1 piece
Bottle gourd (2 inch to 3 inch)	1 piece
Tomatoes	2 medium
Spring onions	3 stems
Fenugreek leaves	1 cup
Mint leaves	1 cup
Ghee	4 tbsps
Onion, finely chopped	1 large
Dhan-saak masala	2 tbsps
Garlic paste	10 cloves
Green chilli paste	4 small
Ginger paste	1inch piece
Salt	to taste
Tamarind water	2-3 tbsps
Coriander leaves	1 tbsp

For the Rice

Ghee	2 tbsps
Onions, finely chopped	2 medium
Cinnamon	2 sticks
Cloves	2
Salt	½ tsp
Sugar	3 tsps
Uncooked rice, washed and soaked	2 cups
Water	4 cups

To Serve

Onion and Tomato Salad

METHOD

FOR DHAN-SAAK

1. Mix all the grams and wash them. Cut potatoes, brinjal, bottle gourd, tomatoes, and spring onions into big pieces. Wash fenugreek and mint leaves.
2. Add all this to a pressure cooker with seven cups of water. Let it cool and liquidize and sieve the mixture. Heat *ghee* in a saucepan and fry chopped onion, until soft.
3. Add *dhan-saak masala* and ginger-vegetable, chilli-garlic paste. Fry for three to four minutes. Add the cooked gram mixture, salt, tamarind water. Bring to a boil. Serve hot with brown rice.

FOR THE RICE

1. Heat *ghee* in a skillet, fry onions, cinnamon, cloves, garlic and fry for two minutes. Add the rice, salt and water.
2. Cook sugar separately with one teaspoon of water, when it turns brown; add to the rice while it is still cooking. Simmer till the rice is soft. Serve hot with *dhan-saak*.

Serves 4-6

ONION AND TOMATO SALAD

Mix together one thinly sliced onion and tomato, two small chopped green chillies, one tablespoon of finely chopped coriander, one tablespoon of vinegar, one teaspoon of each salt and sugar. Serve chilled with *dhan-saak*.

SITAFAL BASUNDI
Custard Apple Dessert

++

INGREDIENTS

Full fat milk .... 1½ litres	A pinch of cardamom powder
Sugar .... 6 tbsps	**To Garnish**
Custard apple pulp .... 1 cup	Toasted and sliced pistachios

METHOD

1. Heat the milk with sugar on a slow flame, stirring time to time until sugar has melted.
2. Put it on a medium heat and boil until it reduces to half.
3. During this process, don't stir but scrape of the milk fat, which gathers on the sides.
4. Remove from heat and cool completely. Add the custard apple pulp and mix well.
5. Chill for two hours. Garnish with pistachios and serve.

Note: _Any other fruit can be replaced for custard apple. i.e. Peach, mango, orange, kiwi, etc._

Serves 4-6

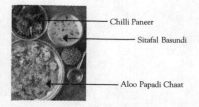

— Chilli Paneer

— Sitafal Basundi

— Aloo Papadi Chaat

MIXED VEGETABLE CURRY

++

INGREDIENTS

French beans	½ kg	
Green peas	½ kg	
Potatoes	½ kg	
Cauliflower	½ kg	
Spring onions	1 bunch	
Ghee	100 gms	
Curry leaves	5-6 pieces	
Curry powder	2 tbsps	
Thick coconut milk	4 cups	
Tomatoes, cut into pieces	750 gms	
Tamarind water	3 tbsps	
Salt	to taste	

For the Paste

Dry red chillies, soaked in water .... 8-10 pieces
Ginger .... 1 inch piece
Peanuts .... ½ cup
Almonds or cashews .... ¼ cup
Freshly grated coconut .... 1 cup
Cumin seeds .... 1 tsp
Garlic .... 20 cloves
Water .... ¼ cup

To Serve

Onion-Tomato Salad and steamed rice

To Garnish

Finely chopped coriander leaves.

METHOD

1. Cut French beans into two inch strips.
2. Shell green peas.
3. Peel and cut potatoes into quarters.
4. Cut cauliflower into small florettes.
5. Cut spring onions into one inch pieces. Liquidize tomatoes in the blendeer and pass it through a sieve.
6. Make a smooth paste of all the ingredients for the paste.
7. Heat *ghee* in a thick vessel and fry curry leaves and onions until brown.
8. Add the paste and curry powder, fry until fragrant. Add a likttle water if required.
9. Add the prepared vegetables and spring onions.
10. Mix well until coated with the paste. Cook until vegetables are soft. Add little water to prevent them from sticking.
11. Add liquidized tomatoes, tamarind water and salt.
12. Bring to a boil and simmer until gravy is thick.
13. Add the coconut milk and adjust the salt.
14. Simmer for five to ten minutes. Garnish with coriander leaves and serve hot with steamed rice and onion-tomato salad.

Serves 8-10

SPINACH SEV-PURI

INGREDIENTS

...nach leaves, washed and cut into 2 inch circle
.... 15-20 pieces
...toes, cubed and boiled .... 2 medium
...n, finely chopped .... 1 small
...t and sour chutney .... ½ cup
...c chutney .... ½ cup
...ev .... ½ cup
.... for frying

For the batter
Gram flour .... ¼ cup
Water .... ¼ cup
Salt .... ½ tsp
Chilli powder .... ½ tsp
Lemon juice .... ½ tsp
Oregano seeds .... ½ tsp
A pinch of asafoetida and fruit salt

METHOD

...all the ingredients for the batter and beat until smooth. Set aside for thirty minutes.
...n spinach leaves and dip each one in the prepared batter and fry in hot oil, two to three at a...
... until crisp. Drain on kitchen paper. Allow it to cool.
...ge five to six of fried spinach *puries* on a plate. Place three to four potato cubes on each one...
...ed by chopped onion.
...oth the *chutney* as per your taste.
...e sev and coriander leaves and serve right away.

Serves 4

CHEESE PAPAD ROLL

INGREDIENTS

Moong *papads* (thin variety) .... 4 pieces
Processed cheese, cut into 1 inch sticks. 250 gms

Chilli powder .... 1 tsp
Oil .... for frying

METHOD

1. Place *papad* on the working surface and make it wet with just enough water to soften it. Cut each one into one inch strips.
2. Place one cheese stick on the edge of the *papad* strip and lightly roll it. Secure ends with a toothpick. Holding one end of the toothpick, fry in hot oil.
3. Remove and drain on paper towel. Sprinkle chilli powder. Repeat this for the remaining *papads*.

Serves 6

HARA-BHARA CHAAT
Green Gram Snack

INGREDIENTS

Oil .... 1 tbsp
Cumin seeds .... ½ tsp
Green chillies, slit 1-2
Curry leaves 1-2
Fresh green grams .... 250 gms
Shelled green peas .... 250 gms
Black salt .... to taste
Salt .... to taste
Lemon juice .... to taste
Dried mango powder .... 1 tbsp

Mint chutney .... ¼ cup
Tomato finely chopped .... 1 medium
Onion finely chopped .... 1 medium
Finely chopped coriander .... 1 tbsp
Chopped green chillies .... 1 tbsp
Spinach sev .... 100 gms
A pinch of soda-bi-carbonate
To Serve
Potato baskets or tart cases

METHOD

1. Heat oil in a saucepan, fry cumin seeds and chilli. Add grams and peas with a pinch of soda-bi-carbonate. Sprinkle little water to avoid sticking.
2. Cook uncovered until soft. Add black salt, salt and mango powder. Mix well. Just before serving mix mint chutney, tomato, onion, coriander and chopped green chillies.
3. Spoon this mixture in a tart case or a potato basket. Garnish with spinach sev and serve.

Makes 12 appetizer portions

PARTY MIX

INGREDIENTS

Peanuts	½ cup	Popcorn	100 gms
Roasted grams	½ cup	Chaat masala	1 tbsp
Fried Bengal grams	½ cup	Chilli powder	1 tbsp
Fried small papads	100 gms	Dry mango powder	1 tbsp
Potato straws	100 gms	Black salt	1 tsp
Lotus puffs	100 gms	Cumin powder	1 tsp
Sago wafers	100 gms	Sesame seeds	1 tsp
Poha wafers	100 gms	Salt and sugar	to taste
Sliced coconut	100 gms	Oil	2-3 tbsps

METHOD

1. In a wide pan, heat oil and add peanuts, roasted gram and fried gram. Fry for two to three minutes. Mix all the spices in a small bowl.
2. Add the remaining ingredients in turn along with the spices, salt and sugar. Remove from stove and set aside to cool. Store in an airtight container.

Makes approximately 1 kg

BAJARI UTTAPAM
Millet Pancake

INGREDIENTS

Whole millet grains, soaked	¼ cup	Garlic paste	2 tbsps
Millet flour	1 cup	Salt	to taste
Yogurt	½ cup	Banana leaves	8-10 (5x5 square)
Onion, diced	1 medium	Oil	for frying
Tomato, diced	1 medium	**To Serve**	
Ginger paste	2 tbsps	Green chutney and fried green chillies (recipe on
Chilli paste	2 tbsps	page 19)	

METHOD

1. Cook millet grains in a pressure cooker. Mix millet flour and yogurt in a bowl to a smooth batter. Cover and set aside for one to two hours.
2. Just before making the pancake, add chilli-ginger-garlic paste, diced onion and tomato and salt to taste. If you find the batter too thick, add a little water. Heat a flat griddle, coat it with little oil.
3. Apply little oil on the banana leaves, place one leaf on a hot griddle and spread two to three tablespoon of the prepared batter. Smoothen the surface.
4. Sprinkle with millet grains and cover it with another leaf. Let it cook on a medium flame, turn it over and cook again on the other side. Serve hot with green chutney and chillies.

Makes 6-8 pancakes

ALOO-PAPADI CHAAT
Potato and Crispies Snack With Yogurt

INGREDIENTS

Potatoes, boiled, peeled and cut into cubes	2 medium	Finely chopped coriander leaves	
		Thick yogurt, beaten and sieved	
Chickpeas, soaked, boiled and drained	½ cup	Salt	
Crisp puris	250 gms	Chilli powder	
Fine sev	250 gms	Chaat masala	
Salted bundi	100 gms	Roasted cumin powder	
Sweet chutney (recipe given below)	1 cup		

METHOD

1. This snack is individually made. Take six to seven puries per person. Arrange bowl.
2. Layer with potatoes, chickpeas, three to four tablespoons of yogurt, all the s and coriander.
3. Garnish with sev and bundi. Serve at once. Repeat for the remaining papdis.

FOR SWEET CHUTNEY

1. Cook 200 gms of dates and a walnut sized tamarind, two cups of water, powder to taste in a pressure cooker for two to three whistles. Cool.
2. Put the chutney in liquidizer jar and sieve. If you find chutney a littl minutes until thick. Use as required.

(See photo on page 124)

CHEESE PAPAD ROLL

+++

INGREDIENTS

Moong *papads* (thin variety) .... 4 pieces   Chilli powder .... 1 tsp
Processed cheese, cut into 1 inch sticks . 250 gms   Oil .... for frying

METHOD

1. Place *papad* on the working surface and make it wet with just enough water to soften it. Cut each one into one inch strips.
2. Place one cheese stick on the edge of the *papad* strip and lightly roll it. Secure ends with a toothpick. Holding one end of the toothpick, fry in hot oil.
3. Remove and drain on paper towel. Sprinkle chilli powder. Repeat this for the remaining *papads*.

Serves 6

HARA-BHARA CHAAT
Green Gram Snack

+++

INGREDIENTS

Oil .... 1 tbsp   Mint chutney .... ¼ cup
Cumin seeds .... ½ tsp   Tomato finely chopped .... 1 medium
Green chillies, slit 1-2   Onion finely chopped .... 1 medium
Curry leaves 1-2   Finely chopped coriander .... 1 tbsp
Fresh green grams .... 250 gms   Chopped green chillies .... 1 tbsp
Shelled green peas .... 250 gms   Spinach sev .... 100 gms
Black salt .... to taste   A pinch of soda-bi-carbonate
Salt .... to taste   **To Serve**
Lemon juice .... to taste   Potato baskets or tart cases
Dried mango powder .... 1 tbsp

METHOD

1. Heat oil in a saucepan, fry cumin seeds and chilli. Add grams and peas with a pinch of soda-bi-carbonate. Sprinkle little water to avoid sticking.
2. Cook uncovered until soft. Add black salt, salt and mango powder. Mix well. Just before serving mix mint chutney, tomato, onion, coriander and chopped green chillies.
3. Spoon this mixture in a tart case or a potato basket. Garnish with spinach sev and serve.

Makes 12 appetizer portions

PARTY MIX

+++++++++++++++++++++++++++++

INGREDIENTS

Peanuts	½ cup	Popcorn	100 gms
Roasted grams	½ cup	*Chaat masala*	1 tbsp
Fried Bengal grams	½ cup	Chilli powder	1 tbsp
Fried small *papads*	100 gms	Dry mango powder	1 tbsp
Potato straws	100 gms	Black salt	1 tsp
Lotus puffs	100 gms	Cumin powder	1 tsp
Sago wafers	100 gms	Sesame seeds	1 tsp
Poha wafers	100 gms	Salt and sugar	to taste
Sliced coconut	100 gms	Oil	2-3 tbsps

METHOD

1. In a wide pan, heat oil and add peanuts, roasted gram and fried gram. Fry for two to three minutes. Mix all the spices in a small bowl.
2. Add the remaining ingredients in turn along with the spices, salt and sugar. Remove from stove and set aside to cool. Store in an airtight container.

Makes approximately 1 kg

BAJARI UTTAPAM
Millet Pancake

+++

INGREDIENTS

Whole millet grains, soaked	¼ cup	Garlic paste	2 tbsps
Millet flour	1 cup	Salt	to taste
Yogurt	½ cup	Banana leaves	8-10 (5x5 square)
Onion, diced	1 medium	Oil	for frying
Tomato, diced	1 medium	**To Serve**	
Ginger paste	2 tbsps	Green chutney and fried green chillies (recipe on
Chilli paste	2 tbsps	page 19)

METHOD

1. Cook millet grains in a pressure cooker. Mix millet flour and yogurt in a bowl to a smooth batter. Cover and set aside for one to two hours.
2. Just before making the pancake, add chilli-ginger-garlic paste, diced onion and tomato and salt to taste. If you find the batter too thick, add a little water. Heat a flat griddle, coat it with little oil.
3. Apply little oil on the banana leaves, place one leaf on a hot griddle and spread two to three tablespoon of the prepared batter. Smoothen the surface.
4. Sprinkle with millet grains and cover it with another leaf. Let it cook on a medium flame, turn it over and cook again on the other side. Serve hot with green chutney and chillies.

Makes 6-8 pancakes

ALOO-PAPADI CHAAT
Potato and Crispies Snack With Yogurt
+++

INGREDIENTS

Potatoes, boiled, peeled and cut into cubes........ ....2 medium	Finely chopped coriander leaves .... ¼ cup
	Thick yogurt, beaten and sieved .... 2 cups
Chickpeas, soaked, boiled and drained ..... ½ cup	Salt .... to taste
Crisp *puris* .... 250 gms	Chilli powder .... to taste
Fine *sev* .... 250 gms	Chaat masala.. to taste
Salted *bundi* .... 100 gms	Roasted cumin powder .... to taste
Sweet *chutney* (recipe given below) .... 1 cup	

METHOD

1. This snack is individually made. Take six to seven *puries* per person. Arrange them in a shallow bowl.
2. Layer with potatoes, chickpeas, three to four tablespoons of yogurt, all the spices, sweet chutney and coriander.
3. Garnish with *sev* and *bundi*. Serve at once. Repeat for the remaining *papdis*.

Serves 4-6

FOR SWEET CHUTNEY

1. Cook 200 gms of dates and a walnut sized tamarind, two cups of water, salt, black salt and chilli powder to taste in a pressure cooker for two to three whistles. Cool.
2. Put the *chutney* in liquidizer jar and sieve. If you find *chutney* a little thin, boil for five to ten minutes until thick. Use as required.

Makes 1 ½ cups

(See photo on page 124)

SPINACH SEV-PURI

INGREDIENTS

Spinach leaves, washed and cut into 2 inch circle
.... 15-20 pieces
Potatoes, cubed and boiled .... 2 medium
Onion, finely chopped .... 1 small
Sweet and sour chutney .... ½ cup
Garlic chutney .... ½ cup
Fine sev .... ½ cup
Oil ....for frying

For the batter
Gram flour .... ¼ cup
Water .... ¼ cup
Salt .... ½ tsp
Chilli powder .... ½ tsp
Lemon juice .... ½ tsp
Oregano seeds .... ½ tsp
A pinch of asafoetida and fruit salt

METHOD

1. Mix all the ingredients for the batter and beat until smooth. Set aside for thirty minutes.
2. Drain spinach leaves and dip each one in the prepared batter and fry in hot oil, two to three at a time, until crisp. Drain on kitchen paper. Allow it to cool.
3. Arrange five to six of fried spinach *puries* on a plate. Place three to four potato cubes on each one followed by chopped onion.
4. Pour both the *chutney* as per your taste.
5. Sprinkle sev and coriander leaves and serve right away.

Serves 4

130

MANGO SQUASH

+++

INGREDIENTS

Alphonso mango pulp, sieved (approx. 10 mangoes) .... 1 litre

Sugar .... 1 kg (approx)

Water .... 1 litre

Citric acid .... 2 tbsps

Sodium benzoite (optional) .... ½ tsp

Potassium Meta bi sulphate (optional) ...... ½ tsp

METHOD

1. Measure mango juice with a cup measure. Take same quantity of sugar. Mix it with water and put it to boil. Add citric acid when sugar has completely melted.

2. Boil it for three to four minutes further and remove from heat. Strain the sugar syrup and set aside to cool. Add sieved mango pulp to this syrup and mix well.

3. If you are using the preservative, mix the powder in a little of the juice and add it to the mixture. Fill in glass bottles and store in the refrigerator.

4. Use three to four tablespoons of this squash mixed with three-fourth glass of cold water and ice to get one glass of mango squash.

Note: *To get smooth drink, mix the squash and water with a rod blender before putting the ice.*

Make 20 glasses

SHIKANJI
Sweetened Lemon Water

+++++++++++++++++++++++++++

INGREDIENTS

Fresh lemon 2

Sugar .... 3-4 tbsps

Salt .... a small pinch

Saffron, powdered .... 4-5 strands

Water .... 2 cups

To Serve

Ice cubes

METHOD

1. Squeeze juice of lemon and mix with sugar and salt until sugar has melted.
2. Add little water and saffron. Mix well.
3. Add remaining water and pour out in two tall glasses filled with ice.

Serves 2

LEMON SNOW MIST

INGREDIENTS

Whipping cream .... 1 cup	Corn flour ....4 tbsps
Sprite or lemonade .... 500 ml	Butter ....1 tbsp
Sugar .... ¾ cup	*For Lemon Curd*
Lemon juice .... 4 tbsps	Cold milk .... 1½ cups

METHOD

FOR LEMON CURD

1. Mix all the ingredients for lemon curd in a saucepan and heat gently, stirring continuously. Remove from heat when the mixture is thick and transparent.
2. Set aside to cool. Whip the cream until soft peaks. Fold it in the lemon curd when it is completely cool. Mix well. Freeze this mixture for three to four hours or over night.
3. Take a tall pilsner glass and put a scoop of frozen lemon cream. Top it up with chilled sprite.
4. Add the sprite gently to avoid the froth overflowing. Serve with a straw.

Serves 4

COCONUT REFRESHER

INGREDIENTS

Drinking coconuts .... 2 pieces	*To Garnish*
Sugar .... 2 tsps	A few red rose petals
Finely diced apple, sprinkled with half a tsp of	A small pinch of salt
lemon juice ....½ cup	Splashes of grenadine syrup

METHOD

1. Chill the coconuts in their shells thoroughly. Remove water and the flesh from them.
2. Blend together with sugar in a liquidizer till all the flesh is incorporated with water. Add a pinch of salt.
3. Pour out in individual glasses, splash grenadine syrup, decorate with rose petals and serve.

Serves 4

NAVRATNA RABRI

Thickened Milk with Nine Jewels

+++

INGREDIENTS

Milk .... 1½ litre	Chopped dry fruits (almonds, cashew, pistachios,
Saffron .... a few strands	glace cherries and dates) .... ½ cup
Sugar .... 8 tbsps	Chopped fresh fruit (apples, oranges, strawberies
Cardamom powder .... ½ tsp	and grapes) .... ¾ cup

METHOD

1. Boil milk on low flame till reduced to half. Keep pushing cream that forms on top of the milk to the sides of the pan.
2. Mix saffron in little milk and add it to hot milk along with sugar, cardamom powder and dry fruits. Cook for two to three minutes.
3. Remove from heat and cool at room temperature. Add fresh fruits and mix well. Transfer to a serving dish and chill before serving.

Serves 6

GLOSSARY
+++++++++++++++++

Achaar	–	Brine pickle
Asafoetida	–	Pungent spice obtained from a plant, believed to aid digestion, should be used in small quantities.
Amba Haldi	–	White turmeric root, used to flavour vegetable
Ajwain	–	Carum seeds, small light brown colour and have bitter flavouring and has digestive properties.
Bottle gourd	–	Dudhi, a white coloured pulpy vegetable.
Bay leaf	–	Tej patta, leaf of the cassia tree, most widely used aromatic herbs, is also on cinnamon family.
Caraway seeds	–	known as Shahjeera- dark brown very small seeds, used for falvouring breads and vegetable dishes.
Curry powder	–	A mixture of a few spices like cinnamon, coriander, cumin, cardamom, pepper etc. roasted and ground to a powder. Used widely not only in south India but all over the world to prepared curries.
Curry leaves	–	Aromatic dark green leaves used mainly for tempering.
Cardamom	–	Intensely aromatic 15-20 black seeds enclosed in straw coloured pod, used for subtle flavour in spice mixture or sweet dishes.
Cloves	–	A small brown, nail shaped spice that emits spicy fragrance.
Cinnamon	–	Fragrant bark of a tree in stick form with a strong aroma and used as a spice.
Chilli/chilli powder	–	Green or red spicy and pungent, used as whole or paste or powdered spice.
Cumin seeds	–	Pale brown or black seeds used as spice with sweetish taste.
Coriander leaves/seeds	–	Leaves are aromatic herb, its leaves and stems are used for flavour in dishes or for garnish on top and the seeds are whole or powdered form used in many spice mixtures, savouries and pickles.
Chaat masala	–	A spicy piquant combination of salty, tart and pungent tastes, widely used in snacks.
Cottage cheese	–	Paneer, Indian cottage cheese, made by curdling the milk.
Dried mango powder	–	Raw, sour mangoes are peeled, cut into pieces and dried in the sun and then powdered. This is used for tangy and sour taste to many dishes.
Dhan-saak masala	–	Blend of aromatic spices to give distinctive flavour to this medley of grams and vegetable curry.

Drumsticks	–	Sahijan or saragva ni singh or shegat ki falli, the long ridged pods, contain firm grayish pulp.
Fenugreek leaves/seeds	–	Methi leaves as it is called in India, have slightly bitter flavour used both as herb as well as vegetable, but the seeds have a very strong smell and are used in small quantities for tempering.
Garam masala	–	Mixture of many hot spices ground together to give a dish subtle taste. It can be ground and stored in a jar to used year round.
Ginger	–	It is a rhizome, with a likeable pungent flavour, used widely in Indian cooking. Also available in dry form.
Gol/Gud	–	Jaggery, a solid lump of unrefined sugar with a unique flavour made from sugarcane.
Ghee	–	Clarified butter, used in many Indian dishes as a cooking medium. Home made ghee has a special flavour, which is made by simmering butter in a thick vessel until ghee separates leaving residue at the bottom.
Grams	–	Pulses-dals, whole or split. Kinds of grams are listed below:
Chickpeas	–	Kabuli channa or chole, Red split gram- Tuvar dal, Yellow split gram - Moong dal without skin, Green gram - Mung, Bengal gram split - Chana dal, Black/white gram - Whole udad or udad dal, Kidney beans - Rajma, Field beans - Val. Orange split gram - Masoor dal.
Gram flour	–	Besan, powdered begal grams or chickpeas, used for batter as well as thickening of gravies.
Jeeralu powder	–	Cumin based, dry mixture of spices used to add extra salty and spicy flavour to the food.
Kasuri methi	–	Dried fenugreek leaves, used to enhance the flavour of the gravies.
Kokam	–	Garcinia indica, it's a dark purple coloured acidic fruit used to give sour taste to curries and pulses.
Lemon	–	Very extensively used in Indian cuisines. It makes refreshing drink with sugar and water, used for sour flavouring or in pickles.
Millet	–	Bajra/jawar, pearl like seed. A kind of cereal, dark and white, two types, used as staple food in many dry hot parts of India.
Mace	–	Jawintri, orange coloured membrane of nutmeg, powdered and sparingly used for sweet as well as savory flavour.
Mustard leaves/seeds	–	Tiny reddish brown/black seeds, commonly used for tempering. Mustard leaves have very pungent taste and used as vegetable.
Nigella seeds	–	Kalonji or onion seeds, used as flavouring for snacks or pickles.

Poppy seeds	–	Khus-khus, tiny cream coloured seeds, used as seeds or in form of paste for curry dishes.
Pomegranate seeds	–	Dried seeds of pomegranate give tangy flavour and dark colour to the dishes.
Parval	–	Cylindrical shaped, very tasty Indian vegetable with hard skin and white pulp.
Papdi	–	Kind of broad green beans, small and big variety used widely in vegetable dishes.
Papads	–	Paper thin crisp rounds, prepared from gram, vegetables or grain with spices and salt. Eaten as an accompaniment to a meal or as a snack.
Ridge gourd	–	Turia, a vegetable from gourd family, with thick ridged skin and dark green colour.
Raita	–	Salad like combination of yogurt and different types of raw or cooked vegetables, flavoured with spices.
Saffron	–	Kesar, most expensive spice, it imparts very pleasing flavour as well as golden colour, used as flavouring for rice dishes as well as sweets.
Sesame seeds	–	Beige coloured unpolished seeds with a nutty flavour, commonly used in Indian cooking.
Semolina		Cream of wheat.
Sev		Vermicelli savoury snack.
Shallots		Small variety of onions with mild flavour.
Shahjeera		Black cumin seeds with subtle flavour.
Tamarind	–	Ripe tamarind which is brown in colour, used widely to add sour taste to vegetables, snacks and chutneys. Usually used by soaking in water and extracting pulp.
Turmeric	–	Haldi, bright yellow powder, used as spice or fresh root used in tempering or pickling.
Tendli	–	Oval shaped green Indian vegetable.
Tandoori masala	–	A special blend of aromatic spices used to marinade vegetables or meat for grilling and barbecuing.
Varakh		Silver or gold leaf, used to garnish sweet dishes.
Yam	–	Root vegetable brown or pink variety, has bland flavour.